DO WHAT
MATTERS
MOST

DO WHAT MATTERS MOST

LEAD WITH A VISION, MANAGE WITH A PLAN, PRIORITIZE YOUR TIME

ROB SHALLENBERGER &
STEVE SHALLENBERGER

Berrett–Koehler Publishers, Inc

Berrett-Koehler Publishers, Inc.
1333 Broadway, Suite 1000
Oakland, CA 94612-1921
Tel: (510) 817-2277
Fax: (510) 817-2278
www.bkconnection.com

ORDERING INFORMATION
Quantity sales. Special discounts are available on quantity purchases by corporations, associations, and others. For details, contact the "Special Sales Department" at the Berrett-Koehler address above.
Individual sales. Berrett-Koehler publications are available through most bookstores. They can also be ordered directly from Berrett-Koehler: Tel: (800) 929-2929; Fax: (802) 864-7626; www.bkconnection.com.
Orders for college textbook / course adoption use. Please contact Berrett-Koehler: Tel: (800) 929-2929; Fax: (802) 864-7626.

Distributed to the U.S. trade and internationally by Penguin Random House Publisher Services.

Berrett-Koehler and the BK logo are registered trademarks of Berrett-Koehler Publishers, Inc.

Printed in the United States of America.

Berrett-Koehler books are printed on long-lasting acid-free paper. When it is available, we choose paper that has been manufactured by environmentally responsible processes. These may include using trees grown in sustainable forests, incorporating recycled paper, minimizing chlorine in bleaching, or recycling the energy produced at the paper mill.

Unless otherwise noted all images and illustrations are copyright © Becoming Your Best Global Leadership.

Roles and Goals® and Pre-week Planning® are registered trademarks of Becoming Your Best Global Leadership.

Library of Congress Cataloging-in-Publication Data
Names: Shallenberger, Robert R., author. | Shallenberger, Steven R., author.
Title: Do what matters most : lead with a vision, manage with a plan, prioritize your time / Rob Shallenberger & Steve Shallenberger.
Description: First edition. | Oakland, CA : Berrett-Koehler Publishers, Inc., [2021] | Includes bibliographical references and index.
Identifiers: LCCN 2021001487 | ISBN 9781523092574 (paperback) | ISBN 9781523092581 (adobe pdf) | ISBN 9781523092598 (epub)
Subjects: LCSH: Time management. | Goal (Psychology) | Performance. | Success in business.
Classification: LCC HD69.T54 S53 2021 | DDC 658.4/09—dc23
LC record available at https://lccn.loc.gov/2021001487

First Edition
27 26 25 24 23 22 21   10 9 8 7 6 5 4 3 2 1

Book producer and text designer: Happenstance Type-O-Rama
Cover designer: Irene Morris

This book is dedicated to the many friends and family members who have deeply influenced our lives, especially Roxanne and Tonya. In addition, it is dedicated to each of Steve's children—David, Steven, Tommy, Daniel, and Anne (and their amazing spouses)—and Rob's children—Robbie, Bella, Lana, and Clara.

CONTENTS

PREFACE

One of the common threads that bind so many people together is a desire to make a difference, be more productive, perform at a higher level, and prioritize what matters most in their lives. People are searching for a way to stay ahead of the curve and do what matters most, whether that means being productive in the office or focusing on their health, their relationships, or their own well-being. The challenge is that most people simply do not have a process or a place to start and are left instead feeling frustrated. Global events such as pandemics and natural disasters can magnify these challenges; for example, you might be working from home while still balancing childcare, or you might be trying to deal with everything on your plate while not being in the same office with the rest of your team.

When it comes to performance and productivity, most organizations and leaders are thirsting for something that will help them prioritize their time and do what matters most. Employees are often asked to do more with less, which results in frustration, turnover, and a suboptimal culture. Leaders are trying to figure out how to improve results and profitability within their division or department, but often they are not sure what else to try.

In our research of more than 1,260 managers and executives from more than 108 different organizations, 68 percent of them felt like their number one challenge was how to prioritize their time. At the same time, 80 percent did not have a process to plan or focus on what matters most.

Steve and Rob have invested decades of research to identify the high-performance habits of the top 10 percent across industries to find something that will help close the productivity gap. In this book, we share three specific habits that increase performance and productivity by at least 30 to 50 percent while at the same time reducing stress. This translates into teams of people who get things done on time or ahead of schedule; who are better contributors, better leaders, and more actively engaged; who do what matters most; and who improve their personal lives and relationships.

The three high performance habits Steve and Rob identified are to develop a written personal vision, to identify and set roles and goals, and to consistently do pre-week planning. People have heard a lot about these three habits throughout their lives, but most people are still not doing them. In fact, only 2 percent of people have a written personal vision, less than 10 percent feel confident in writing goals (or have written goals), and 80 percent don't feel they have a process to effectively plan their weeks.

We train private, public, and government organizations around the world and have seen firsthand the impact these three habits have on employees and leaders. From the CEO to the frontline employee, we have seen massive improvements in people when they focus on these three habits. These are not flavors of the month; rather, these three habits transform a person's focus for the rest of their lives. We have taken years of training and compiled it in this book so that managers and employees have a simple yet extremely effective place to start.

Although this book is primarily written for employees, managers, and executives in both the private and public sectors, the same habits equally affect a student, an athlete, a teenager, and anyone else who applies them. It is common to have parents give this book to their son or daughter because the same habits that are significant for members of an organization are just as important for a daughter, son, or student.

Do what matters most is both a mindset and a skillset that will affect every area of a person's life. We invite you to test these powerful habits in your life as well as share them with the people who you care most about. After reading this book, you will be able to test firsthand how effective these habits are for you, your coworkers, and your family!

INTRODUCTION

How to Increase Productivity by 30 to 50 Percent

Amy (all names throughout the book have been changed to protect the privacy of the actual person) was a rising star at American Express. Through the years, she excelled at what she did and was promoted over and over again until she became a senior director. After some time in this role, she began to feel as if something was missing in her life, but she was not quite sure what it was. It was something intangible that she couldn't quite put her finger on. She described it as feeling as if she had reached a plateau combined with being overwhelmed by all the pressures and deadlines of her new leadership role. She felt that she was no longer prioritizing what mattered most, and it seemed as if she was always in reaction mode.

Amy was in her forties, so for a while, she brushed these feelings off as being something normal for her age. Her initial response was to work harder and put more effort into the seemingly endless list of projects at work. She thought she could solve the problem by focusing, working harder, and finishing some of the big projects. However, weeks turned into months, and nothing changed. Her attention would drift and her energy would wane as each day wore on. Even though she worked harder, she felt she was less productive, and the pile of tasks didn't seem to get any smaller. Her supervisor, a senior leader, commented that it seemed like Amy's attitude and demeanor had shifted, as well as her productivity. This conversation with her boss only contributed to Amy's feelings of being overwhelmed and frustrated.

It was not just work; she felt her relationships with her husband, her daughter, and even some of her friends were slipping as well. She now understood what it meant to "bring work home" after a long day. Her daughter was born with a challenging disease, and she felt she was not giving her daughter the time she deserved. As if the frustrations in her work and home life were not enough, she also felt as if she didn't have time to take care of herself. For example, she was not getting the exercise she used to.

She used words like *overwhelmed*, *frustrated*, and *in a rut* to describe how she felt. How did this happen? How did this rising star get to a place where she felt this way?

Amy was not the type of person to roll over and give up; she was committed to getting things back on track. However, when it came to productivity and time-management, she quickly discovered a lot of noise and conflicting information. Amy read various books and listened to different podcasts looking for solutions. Through the subsequent months, she tried a lot of different things that she picked up from various sources. She found some tips: Start with the most significant project first thing in the morning. Identify your three big goals for the day and focus on those. Amy found these to be good advice, but none of them solved her fundamental problem—the most important things were not happening for her, and she could not get out of this productivity rut. She was searching for a framework or a process that would help her be meaningfully productive, make time for what mattered most, and get her internal fire back.

It was at this point in her life when we met Amy. She attended a Do What Matters Most keynote at a large training conference in Washington, DC. The keynote focused on what we call *the big three*:

1. How to develop a written personal vision

2. How to set roles and goals

3. How to do pre-week planning

After the keynote ended, Amy briskly walked toward the front of the room. It was apparent that she was on a mission to get to where we were standing. When she reached us, she excitedly shook Rob's hand and said, "This is it! I finally found what I have been looking for . . . a process that is *simple* and will help me get my life back! I have read all kinds of things about vision, goals, and weekly planning, but I have never seen it presented in this way."

She briefly explained her background and all that had happened that year, both personally and professionally. We were excited because she was excited. She had the right mindset; the only thing Amy needed was the skillset to improve performance and productivity. She promised that she would apply the new process of vision, goals, and pre-week planning and then share her results the following month. We knew that if she put in the effort to develop her vision, roles and goals, and if she was consistent about her pre-week planning, it would have a significant impact on every aspect of her life.

True to her word, almost exactly a month later, Amy sent an email that said the following:

> I just wanted to let you know that vision, roles and goals, and pre-week planning really made a lasting impact on me. My boss, peers, and direct reports see a difference in me—that I am more positive and organized than I've been in a long time. Personally, I have lost 10 pounds this month, I've exercised five times a week, and I've recommitted to all the relationships in my life (family, friends, and especially my husband and daughter). I'm finding hours in the day that I never even knew were there, and I've been so productive. These habits changed my life!

Several months after she sent this email, we saw Amy again, and you could see the difference in her demeanor and attitude. Although we were excited to see this lasting change, it was not a surprise to see this turnaround in her life. Once she had a process and a framework, Amy went through a total transformation.

There are a lot of Amys in the world. At some point, we have all been where she was to one degree or another; perhaps we have even accepted our current situation as normal and have done nothing about it.

Like Amy, most people desire to be more productive, to perform at a higher level, to make a difference for good, and to prioritize what matters most in their lives. But most people simply do not have a process or a place to start and are left feeling frustrated.

Global events can magnify these feelings with new challenges. For example, remote work, childcare, and online schooling are all real and valid concerns that are now commonplace throughout the world.

From our experience, we know that countless leaders want to see improvements in the performance and productivity of their team members. Some of the most common questions we hear from people are "Where should I start?" and "What should I do?" To answer that question, we believe that real transformation in performance and productivity requires both a mindset *and* a skillset. In other words, if a person or team wants to see a significant improvement, they need to start with the right mindset and then apply the skillset. In Amy's case, she had the mindset—the willingness and the discipline—to apply the same skillset you will learn in this book. When people have the willingness and discipline to apply the skillset, they will see significant results in their personal and professional lives.

Most people have heard a lot about vision, goals, and some form of weekly planning. Yet, although many have heard these terms, very few have actually applied them—we will share the data later. The specific processes shared in this book will bring vision, goals, and pre-week planning together in a new and unique way. By the end of the book, we hope you will agree that these are presented in a way that is simple, yet life-changing.

How This Book Came About

We have invested more than 40 years researching the top 10 percent of great leaders and high performers across industries. In that research, we have found 12 principles of highly successful people and leaders that you see over and over in the very best. These 12 principles are found in our other book, *Becoming Your Best: The 12 Principles of Highly Successful Leaders*.

Of course, nobody who we researched or interviewed was perfect (none of us are). But, when we saw what high performers focused on, the 12 principles were clearly the common denominator to the success of most of them. These 12 principles are strong predictors of success, both personally and professionally.

After we trained hundreds of organizations focusing on the implementation of the 12 principles, we found that 3 principles always resonated deeply with people around the world—lead with a vision, manage with a plan, and prioritize your time. Although our original book (*Becoming Your Best*) certainly detailed these 3 principles, we knew there was more to be done at the organizational level when it came to planning and productivity. Thus began a new journey of research where we focused on the principles lead with a vision, manage with a plan, and prioritize your time.

Here are a few of the questions we wanted to answer as part of this new research: How many people in an organization had a personal vision? How proficient were employees and managers at setting goals? Was their current goal-setting process working? How did managers and employees prioritize their time and plan their weeks? Was their current approach to weekly planning effective? When teams learned how to effectively set goals and prioritize their time, what affect did that have on their results? How did planning or the lack of planning effect people's stress levels? How could individuals and teams consistently stay ahead of the curve and prioritize what mattered most?

It was these types of questions and our curiosity that led us to take a deeper dive into these three principles. We wanted to build an extension on our first book and conduct more focused research that would transcend race, culture, and gender. We wanted to research organizations to include brand-new startups as well as the most recognizable names. We wanted to accurately find out what impact these three principles had on performance and productivity.

The results of our research clearly conveyed that managers and employees needed something to help them prioritize their time and do what matters most. So, although the original book touched on these three principles, in *Do What Matters Most*, we go significantly deeper into each of them with many more resources, research updates, and tools.

After finalizing our research, we identified three corresponding habits that are key to mastering these principles. From this point forward, we will refer to these three high-performance habits—vision, roles and goals, and pre-week planning—as *the big three*.

These habits come together to create a chemistry of excellence!

The big three make up what we often refer to as the *skillset*. We were amazed to discover that less than 1 percent of the people surveyed had developed this skillset. This means that, when you develop these habits, you join a surprisingly small percentage of people. It is the combination of this skillset and the mindset that can have such a transformational impact on both your personal and professional lives.

These three habits dramatically increase productivity and performance as well as a person's ability to focus on what matters most. It is these habits that help people master the three principles we researched.

The following is a brief description of how the habits of vision, roles and goals, and pre-week planning directly tie into their respective principles:

- **Lead with a vision (the principle).**

  Develop a written personal vision (the habit) that is meaningful and gives you direction or purpose.

- **Manage with a plan (the principle).**

  Set specific roles and goals for this year (the habit) to help you get laser-focused on what matters most so that you can have a balance of success stories across every area of your life.

- **Prioritize your time (the principle).**

  Do what matters most through pre-week planning (the habit). Pre-week planning will help you schedule your priorities rather than prioritize your schedule. In other words, every week, you use this process to do what matters most and connect your goals to the weekly and daily level, both personally and professionally.

Rob was a fighter pilot in the US Air Force for 11 years. During that time, he learned that the air force employs a strategic, operational, and tactical focus. The command level focuses on strategy. Operational plans are usually made at the base level and are focused on how to achieve the strategic intent. The tactical focus is done at the squadron level; in other words, it is where the rubber meets the road to achieve the operational and strategic objectives. We invite you to take the same approach to your personal and professional life by developing a written personal vision (strategic focus), by identifying your roles and goals for the year (operational focus), and by using a process called pre-week planning to do what matters most at the weekly and daily level (tactical focus). These three habits will become integral to developing what we call your *flight plan for life*.

The skillset of the big three is what dramatically increases a focus on what matters most in every area of our lives!

What to Expect

We promise that when you focus on *the big three*—vision, roles and goals, and pre-week planning—your productivity will increase by at least 30 to 50 percent, and you will have one of your best years ever!

Even if challenges arise during the year, which they certainly will, you will be better equipped to face them. Not only this, but you will also do so in a way that gives you power, resilience, and focus.

To say that these three habits will significantly increase productivity and empower you to consistently do the things that matter most in your life is a bold promise. Yet, we have seen it happen in our own lives as well as thousands of others, from senior leaders to frontline employees, and from students to stay-at-home parents.

Imagine what happens to a team when you can take the average employee productivity and increase it by 30 to 50 percent! That often translates into millions of dollars, and even more than that, it results in a productive team filled with people who are fun to work with. Instead of team members who run from fire to fire, you have team members who know how to prioritize their time and do what matters most. Instead of being task saturated, team members communicate well, are responsive, and get things done on or ahead of schedule.

Just as increased productivity is important to the success of any team, it also has a big effect on your personal life. Imagine what can happen in your personal life and relationships when you find hours in the week that you didn't even know were there. Imagine being at your ideal weight or fitness level. Imagine what a great relationship with your partner, spouse, children, or other family members might look like. Imagine waking up in the morning excited to face the day.

Throughout this journey, we will invite you to expand outside your comfort zone, which will take effort on your part. The willingness to stretch and grow is all part of the do what matters most mindset.

Like any endeavor, you will get out of this book what you put into it. There are no shortcuts to success. When you put in the effort, you will see immediate results in both your personal and professional lives. The great part about this skillset is that it does not matter who you are; these habits are time-tested and transcend nationality, race, culture, and gender.

Through the course of this book, our hope is that you will

1. Develop a powerful, written personal vision.

2. Set roles and goals for the year that focus on what matters most.

3. Prioritize your time each week through pre-week planning.

Using these easy-to-understand and straightforward habits, you will learn how to schedule your priorities rather than have your schedule dictate what you do. You will feel the power that comes with a sense of direction and purpose. Stress will decrease and productivity will increase. Your contribution as a leader and team member will increase. You will take care of your physical and mental health and devote more quality time to the important people in your life.

Later in this book, you will see how the application of the big three took an "average" employee and helped her become the top producer on her team; how a senior VP transformed who he was as a leader and reignited his team to achieve record results; how a manager went from always being "busy" and stressed to transforming his team and his home life; how a team member went from taking sick days because of anxiety to significantly improving her sales results; and how a CEO who felt like he'd lost his edge regained his fire and passion.

These are only a few examples of many that you will read about throughout the book. These experiences are from people who saw amazing results when they combined the right mindset with the skillset of the big three. Many of the stories in this book come from people who were already in a good place in life; it was the big three that helped them focus, do what mattered most, and get to an even better place.

This skillset will be a game-changer and one that we hope you will come back to many times throughout your life. We hope you will put in the necessary work and effort to develop these habits and test our promise for yourself.

Take the Personal Productivity Assessment

Before you read the rest of the book, we invite you to go to BYBassessment .com and take a free personal performance and productivity assessment. This assessment will give you an objective score to see how you are doing in different areas of your life. The goal is to improve *your* score and move the needle in *your* life. The objective score translates into subjective results in your day-to-day life.

After you take the assessment, print your results and put them in a place where you can come back to them later. We invite you to retake the assessment in three to four months—after developing the big three habits—and see what your new score is. When you apply what you learn in this book, the score will increase, and you will see considerable improvements in both your personal and professional life. This assessment will identify specific ways to *lead a life by design rather than live a life by default.*

Let's Go!

We are excited for you and grateful that you have made the time to read this book. Although this book is primarily written for employees, managers, and executives, the same habits will equally impact a student, athlete, teenager, and anyone else who applies these habits. Many parents will give this book to their son or daughter because the same habits that are significant for members of an organization are just as important for a daughter, son, or student.

No matter what your title, position, or stage in life, we are confident these habits will have a big impact.

So, let's get started and jump into the do what matters most mindset and skillset!

1

The Do What Matters Most Mindset and Skillset

As mentioned in the introduction, Rob was a fighter pilot for 11 years in the US Air Force. Years ago, Rob was flying an F-16 over South Carolina during a night training mission. He and his wingman were flying at 20,000 feet, and their two jets were about a mile apart. That evening seemed unusually dark, and the only visual frame of reference was the narrow field of view in Rob's night vision goggles. Everything seemed routine until Rob called for a hook turn—a simultaneous 180-degree turn going the same direction—to the left. As he called for the turn, a simulated threat popped up in the radar display over his right knee, which distracted him during the turn. Instead of focusing on the turn and watching his wingman, he shifted his focus to the radar that was displaying the threat. So much was going on in the jet, and without realizing it, he misprioritized what mattered most. That inadvertent mistake almost cost him his life.

What Rob didn't realize was that when he started the 180-degree left-hand turn into his wingman (Rob was on the right side), his wingman mistakenly turned to the right. Without either of them realizing it, they crossed flight paths and missed each other by less than 100 feet travelling at a combined speed of over 1,000 mph.

This hook turn was supposed to be a safe turn in the same direction in which they never got closer than a mile from each other. Yet, so much was happening in the cockpit that Rob lost track of his priorities and nearly died. Unbeknownst to him, something similar was happening in the jet of his wingman. The wingman had a light on in the cockpit that distracted him from his priorities, and he quit watching Rob (the flight lead). In the debrief, while they watched the tapes, both of them breathed a huge sigh of relief when they realized how close they had come to dying.

There is a pilot term called *task saturation*. Task saturation is when a pilot has so many things going on in the cockpit that they are no longer able to process everything. When task saturation creeps in, the pilot starts to *task shed* (drop things from their crosscheck or cockpit scan) and can quickly lose track of their priorities and what matters most. For example, in the cockpit, there are six primary instruments that a pilot should always be aware of, instruments such as altitude and airspeed. Unfortunately, many pilots have crashed because they were task saturated, they misprioritized, and they lost track of their primary instruments—as Rob did that night.

Interestingly, it was not until the debrief that both Rob and his wingman realized how precarious their actual situation had been. During the hook turn, Rob and his wingman should have first ensured their flight path was clear rather than worrying about what was on the radar. Because they were both task saturated, which they didn't realize until the debrief, they misprioritized and focused on the wrong task at the wrong time.

Likewise, the busyness of life ebbs and flows. Although task saturation is extremely obvious sometimes, at other times, a person may not realize they are task saturated and may be lulled into a false sense of complacency. Often it is when people step back to look at their lives (like Rob did in the debrief) that they realize how task saturated they have actually become—it is the act of stepping back that helps them see clearly. Task saturation is insidious, and the most dangerous form of it is when it is unrecognized—as it was with Rob and his wingman that night.

Can you relate to the feeling of task saturation? Surely at some point in your life, you have felt the stress of having so many things coming at you but only having a limited amount of time to accomplish them. When that happens, you likely know what we are talking about when we say that stress increases, performance decreases, and communication (especially effective communication) goes out the window.

The common adage in business now is *do more with less*. This approach to business is a perfect recipe for task saturation and everything that comes with it, such as lower productivity, higher turnover, and a decline in morale. Other feelings associated with task saturation in the workplace include being overwhelmed, upset, frustrated, and perhaps unsure of what you should be doing. When a person is task saturated, it is easy for them to lose track of what matters most. In other words, when a person has too many competing demands for their time, it is common for their priorities to slip through the cracks.

These kinds of performance and productivity challenges are becoming commonplace. It might be a stay-at-home team member who is burned out because they do not have a personal vision. Or, maybe it is a rising leader who has a solid mindset and habits but needs additional tools to do what matters most.

Imagine a pilot who is task saturated and is no longer paying attention to their primary instruments—the ones that will keep them alive. Imagine a leader or team member who is task saturated; how many of their "primary instruments" are likely to slip out of their crosscheck? This demanding environment is why the big three are critical to helping people focus on their primary instruments, or in other words, what matters most.

Phrases that you might hear others say (or maybe you have said them as well) as precursors to task saturation include "I really want to, but I'm just too busy," or "I know I should do that, but I just don't have time." Sometimes, we wear that *busy badge* as a badge of honor—as if busyness equals high productivity. The truth is that when a person is not focused on their priorities and what matters most, it can negatively impact their productivity; their personal well-being, health, and relationships; and even their finances. In fact, being *busy* on the wrong tasks can do far more harm than good—we will explain more in Chapter 2.

There is a direct correlation between performance and productivity and someone's level of task saturation. When task saturation rises, performance almost always decreases. When we talk about performance and productivity, task saturation is just the beginning. The most successful people are the ones whose team members know how to do what matters most and use their time on high-influence activities—in other words, activities that produce the highest return for the time invested. Although that seems obvious, why are time and productivity such enormous challenges for leaders and teams? As mentioned in the introduction, we set out to answer that question.

We have had the opportunity to see behind the curtains in hundreds of global organizations. A common denominator in almost every organization is that most people are busier than ever. It is common for people to feel like they are running from fire to fire or are endlessly chasing the next shiny object yet are never able to catch it. Leaders have an enormous opportunity to help their employees focus on what matters most and use their time on high-influence activities that contribute to the growth and well-being of the organization.

One of the most common questions is this: "Where should I start?" We believe the answer is that real transformation in performance and productivity requires both a mindset *and* a skillset. In other words, if a person or team wants to see a significant improvement, they must start with the right mindset and follow it by applying the skillset.

The Do What Matters Most Mindset

Developing the right mindset is a journey rather than a destination and almost always requires that a person first look internally.

The do what matters most mindset is described in many ways, and one that resonates with almost everyone is this:

> Successful people have the willingness to get laser-focused on what matters most and the discipline to apply the skillset to achieve it consistently.

The do what matters most mindset is a shift away from reactionary living to proactive or intentional living. It is a willingness to make the time to schedule your priorities rather than letting your schedule dictate your every action. The do what matters most mindset shows the discipline to make the new skillset a part of your weekly habits. We like to define *discipline* as doing the right thing at the right time, regardless of how we feel about it. Discipline is an essential part of the do what matters most mindset.

Another way to look at this mindset is described in one of our favorite quotes attributed to St. Jerome:

> *Good, better, best. Never let it rest.*
> *'Til your good is better, and your better is best.*

It does not matter where you are today or what your starting point looks like. For a lot of people, life may be satisfactory in many ways. For example, you may be considered a "good" manager. However, the do what matters most mindset is you honestly asking yourself, *What can I do to be a better, more productive leader or team member? What can I do to be a better parent, spouse, son/daughter, or brother/sister?* No matter what our starting points are right now (even if things are good), this quote invites us to consider that we can all be better in different areas of our lives.

It is often easy to look at others and think about all the things they need to improve (rather than looking at ourselves). Instead of looking at others, the *good, better, best* quote invites each person to take responsibility for themselves. It means looking in the mirror and honestly asking questions such as *What can I do to be a better member of my team?* or *What can I do to be a better leader?* As soon as people start asking themselves these types of questions, their mindset opens the door to a skillset that can empower and enable them to grow dramatically. Performance, productivity, and well-being all begin to improve. The skillset is exponentially more powerful when coupled with a willing mindset.

One of the best examples to illustrate this mindset comes from a 92-year-old business owner in Kenya. During our workshop, he commented to the entire group, "My best is still ahead! I can't wait to finalize my vision and goals and start doing pre-week planning!" Imagine the tone and culture this leader was setting throughout his organization. He clearly showed that he valued learning and growth. He certainly communicated that he was not complacent or comfortable with where he was—even at 92 years old! This type of mindset is what leadership looks like in any successful organization.

The Enemies of the Do What Matters Most Mindset

Our research shows that many employees and managers often react to the fire of the day—a symptom of task saturation. A transformational leader using this mindset will instead minimize the firefighting and proactively prioritize and plan what matters most. We said *minimize* because unanticipated fires always pop up; however, how many of those fires could we have prevented in the first place if we had used proactive planning? It is easier to proactively plan and stay ahead of the curve when we are not task saturated.

Another common mindset battle that we have all faced to one degree or another is that of *complacency*. In the fighter pilot world, complacency is known as the silent killer. Complacency should be as much of a concern for an organization as it is for a pilot. There is a long list of businesses that got too comfortable where they were and did not pivot when they should have: Blockbuster, Blackberry, and Kodak, just to name a few. Complacency can be recognized by phrases such as "I'm fine the way I am" or "Our current approach is working just fine." The internal feeling associated with complacency is a feeling of comfort or a feeling of being in cruise control. The complacent mindset is dangerous because it often closes the door to the idea that there might be a better way. In our experience, comfort can be one of the greatest hindrances to forward progress because it can often invite the thought, *I'm fine the way I am.*

A third enemy of the do what matters most mindset is an emotion within each of us that we label as the *cynic* or the *skeptic*. Cynicism is a very natural emotion, and it serves as a filter or defensive barrier. Here is what we mean by a filter: What would your life be like if you believed everything you saw and heard every day? Chaos! The cynic or skeptic serves as a filter to wade through all the noise and block out what is not helpful. However, because the world is full of so much noise, many of us have let that natural emotion become a dominant way of thinking. When skepticism becomes dominant, it can quickly become one of the enemies of the do what matters most mindset.

What we invite you to do is acknowledge that internal cynic or skeptic and then set it aside for just a few hours while you read this book. In other words, be open to testing the power of these habits in your life. In the spirit of *good, better, best*, see what impact these habits might have on your productivity and performance.

The last enemy of the do what matters most mindset is *procrastination*. Procrastination is one of the great enemies of success. It is insidious and can creep into any person or culture. We have all experienced it to a degree, and it can be easily recognized in the words, "I'll just do it later."

Regarding procrastination, organizational theorist and author Robert Anthony wisely said, "Waiting is a trap. There will always be reasons to wait—the truth is, there are only two things in life, reasons, and results, and reasons don't count!"

It is critical that you remain vigilant about how task saturation, complacency, procrastination, or cynicism shows up in your personal life and within your team. The do what matters most mindset continually reminds us to keep our guard up to avoid these issues and instead schedule our priorities rather than prioritize our schedule. The skillset of a personal vision, roles and goals, and pre-week planning works to combat the enemies of this mindset.

Henry Mintzberg, a business management professor and author, wrote a classical article titled "The Manager's Job" in the August 1975 issue of the *Harvard Business Review.*[1] He captured the exact mindset we are describing when he said, "The manager is challenged to gain control of his or her own time by turning obligations into advantages and by turning those things he or she wishes to do into obligations. Free time is made, not found. Hoping to leave some time open for contemplations or general planning is tantamount to hoping that the pressures of the job will go away."

It is easy to blame a busy schedule or all the competing demands on our time for a lack of focus or productivity. However, adopting this mindset is showing a willingness to look at how things were done in the past and consider that there might be a better way. Once a person is willing to see if there is a better way, the skillset becomes invaluable!

Stepping Outside Your Comfort Zone

Another way to think about the mindset and how it impacts performance and productivity is to consider the analogy of a rubber band. A rubber band is not designed to sit in a drawer. If it does, it loses its flexibility and becomes brittle. A rubber band is made to be stretched!

Likewise, as humans, we are meant to grow and be stretched. Sometimes, this takes us out of our comfort zone, but when we step outside this zone, massive growth can happen. To begin the stretch, honestly ask yourself what you can do to go from good (where you are today) to better, while continuously seeking to do what matters most in the quest for your best.

The do what matters most mindset and skillset are deeply intertwined. Whether you work in the front line of your organization or are the CEO, applying this powerful skillset will stretch your mindset to help you be a better influencer and leader. The reality is that each of us either chooses to lead a life by design or live a life by default. From an organizational perspective, the culture in a team is the sum of each individual team member. So, if you lead a team of any size, the truth is this culture starts with you—that is leadership. If you take on this leadership mindset, others are likely to follow your lead.

Part of developing the right mindset, individually and as a team, is to set proper expectations. Vince Lombardi, the former coach of the Green Bay Packers, lived the do what matters most mindset. He set the same expectations for his team that we will invite you to set for yourself and your team. Lombardi was said to have told his players:

> *We will relentlessly chase perfection, knowing full well we will not catch it because nothing is perfect. But we will relentlessly chase it because, in the process, we will catch excellence. I am not remotely interested in just being good.*

Vince Lombardi won many championships because he instilled this mindset into his players. Although the aim is perfection, we know we will never get there. But, like Vince Lombardi, we are confident you and your team members will catch "excellence" in the pursuit. For those who approach this book with the right mindset—committing to be willing and disciplined—these habits will help move boulders rather than pebbles.

Here is an example of what happens when a team has the right mindset and is willing to stretch—in other words, they are willing to set aside the cynic and develop the skillset.

A successful energy company in California had been working on these principles and habits for years. One day, their sales team went through a half day of internal training focused on the big three. This team was averaging about 17 sales per day, prior to the training, which was in the "good" category. At the end of the workshop, the trainer invited the team to set a new goal—averaging 34 sales per day. The new goal meant a big jump in sales and would require a different mindset and a new skillset to help the team schedule their priorities and shift their time to high-influence activities—what we call Q2 activities, which we will cover later in the book.

You can probably guess the team's initial responses to the new goal. They said things like "We've only hit 34 sales once before," and "I'm not sure about this; that's a huge jump." You can see in their responses how real the skeptic was in each one of them—these are natural and common types of first responses for most of us. Despite their initial doubt and skepticism, the members of the team were good sports and set 34 as their new sales goal to average throughout the coming month. The next day—after being armed with a new mindset and after applying the new skillset—the sales team had a record day. Their sales manager was ecstatic when she proudly shared with the trainer, "You'll never believe it. Today we just shattered our old record and hit 41 sales!"

A month later, this same manager wrote an email saying, "This has been so amazing. Can you guess what our sales average was this month? Thirty-four sales per day!" The team hit the exact goal they had set a month prior. This story repeats itself over and over when people and teams come with the right mindset and then apply the same skillset you will get in this book.

Do you think this sales team could ever go back to 17 sales a day and be satisfied? No. The bar was reset; once the mental bar (mindset) is reset, there is a new standard. This team caught excellence in the pursuit of perfection, and it meant an additional $2.4 million in revenue for the company. More importantly, for each of the sales reps, it meant more money in their pockets, and their job satisfaction significantly increased.

This same type of mental reset can happen with every one of us, whether it is in our professional results, in our health, relationships, and finances, or in our general well-being. Once the bar is moved, it is difficult ever to go back and be satisfied!

The Do What Matters Most Skillset

The *combination* of the big three—a personal vision, roles and goals, and pre-week planning—makes up the skillset that will help a person take control of their schedule and lead a life by design. When going through the process of developing this skillset, you will be able to step back and look at your life from the 30,000-foot view (vision) and then get specific, down to your weekly and daily actions (pre-week planning), where the rubber meets the road.

As we mentioned in the preface, we researched 1,260 managers and executives from more than 108 different organizations. Sixty-eight percent of them felt that their number one challenge was how to prioritize their time. At the same time, 80 percent did not have a process to plan their weeks and do what matters most. In addition, only 2 percent had a written personal vision, and less than 10 percent had both personal and professional written goals for the year.

When it comes to performance and productivity, most organizations and leaders are thirsting for something that will help them prioritize their time, do what matters most, and solve the task saturation problem. In fact, 84 percent of the people we researched felt that if they had a process to prioritize their time, it would have a big impact on their productivity.

Since 68 percent of people feel like prioritizing their time is their greatest challenge, and yet 80 percent do not have a solution, this is an area that is ripe for organizational improvement when it comes to performance and productivity. We are confident that the big three will close this gap, which is why we promised that this skillset will increase performance and productivity by at least 30 to 50 percent.

In Og Mandino's classic book *The Greatest Salesman in the World*, he wisely said, "The only difference between those who have failed and those who have succeeded lies in the difference of their habits. Good habits are the key to all success. Bad habits are the unlocked door to failure. Thus, the first law I will obey, which precedeth all others is—I will form good habits."[2]

Vision, roles and goals, and pre-week planning are the skillset and habits that are strongly predictive of success. However, like anything, they take discipline and effort, which is the mindset part of the equation.

There is a term we like to use called the *performance average*. Our performance average is the current level of productivity across the different roles in our lives. Regardless of your starting point right now, when you implement these three high-performance habits (the skillset), they will have a tremendous impact on your mindset and everything will seem to improve. Just like the change in the mindset of the sales team that went from averaging 17 sales to 34 sales, your performance average will increase in almost every area of your life.

When your performance average increases, this causes a transformed mindset of what you are capable of, both as a person and as a leader. In other words, once you raise your performance average, the bar is reset, and it is difficult to ever go back and be happy about it. It is the application of the skillset that raises the mindset, which is why mindset and skillset are so closely tied together.

What should you expect from an increased performance average when you develop the skillset of the big three?

- A purpose-driven life
- Improved performance and productivity
- Significant improvement in workplace results
- Better health, improved balance, and peace of mind
- Improved relationships
- Improved finances and more money
- A connection to your true, authentic self
- Improved attitude and sense of accomplishment
- Better leadership and team-player skills

Wrap Up

The fact that you are reading this book already shows that you have a willing mindset. Your willingness to test the power of a personal vision, roles and goals, and pre-week planning will open doors of growth that you may not have even known were there. Just as it was for the sales team that went from 17 to 34 sales, it will be interesting to see what is possible for you, both personally and professionally.

This type of thinking is the spirit of *good, better, best* and the high-performer mindset. It is the combination of the high-performer mindset *and* this skillset that will empower you to fend off task saturation, complacency, the cynic, and procrastination.

Before we get into the skillset of the big three in subsequent chapters, we will first focus on defining the difference between performance and productivity and why the focus on doing what matters most really matters.

REFLECTION QUESTIONS FOR THIS CHAPTER:

1. What areas of your personal and professional life would you like to improve? What is your current mindset toward those areas?

2. As a team member or leader, what are some initial thoughts you have on how to be a better contributor or a more effective leader?

3. What is something you have wanted to do that would take you outside your comfort zone? What has kept you from doing it?

2

Why Doing What Matters Most Matters

Earlier, we said that the big three habits would increase performance and productivity by an average of *at least* 30 to 50 percent. People get excited about that promise because of the impact it will have on the profitability and growth of their companies. However, in the corporate setting, the words *performance* and *productivity* are often used interchangeably as if they meant the same thing. The reality is that they mean two vastly different things, and both are important when it comes to doing what matters most. It is critical to understand the differences between these before we get into the big three habits.

If you were sitting at a table with others and asked them to define *performance* and *productivity*, you would likely hear numerous descriptions. Because there are so many varying definitions, we feel it is essential to clarify what they mean in the professional setting and the context of this book.

The reason we want to clarify what each word means is that people often see a significant increase in results when they focus on both performance *and* productivity. The focus on both helps a person or team do what matters most, and it is exactly what the big three do. We often think of performance and productivity as only a "work" thing, but the reality is that performance and productivity tie into every area of our lives, such as our health, relationships, and emotional well-being.

Let us look at how these are different and yet still deeply intertwined with each other.

Productivity is often measured in terms
of the rate of output per unit of input.[3]

In a hypothetical sales example, imagine that salesperson A works eight hours a day, makes 20 calls, and closes one deal per day. That is a close ratio of 1:20. In this case, productivity is measured by the number of calls made—20 calls per day.

Performance is the ability to do
something efficiently and effectively.[4]

Using the same sales analogy, imagine that salesperson B works the same number of hours, only makes 10 calls, and closes one deal per day. In this case, performance is measured by the close ratio—1:10 (reference Table 1).

Table 1. Current Sales Numbers

	Salesperson A	Salesperson B
Number of calls per day (productivity)	20	10
Close ratio (performance)	1:20	1:10
Total sales per day	1	1

Salesperson A is *producing* (number of calls) at a higher level than salesperson B because she is making more calls per day. Salesperson B is *performing* (close ratio) at a higher level than salesperson A because he has a higher close ratio.

If you are the leader of both salesperson A and B, it might be tempting to look at the total sales per day and say they are producing the same . . . one sale per day. But that would be incorrect because the way they each get to one sale is very different. As a leader, if you are tasked with increasing sales on your team, then you will want to see salesperson A increase her performance (improve the close ratio), and salesperson B increase his productivity (make more calls). Then you should start to see massive results with the focus on both performance *and* productivity.

As the leader of these two salespeople, what is the impact if you can get salesperson A to increase her *performance* by improving her close ratio from 1:20 to 1:10? In this example, her sales would increase by 100 percent.

Salesperson B already has a close ratio of 1:10 while only making 10 calls per day. As his leader, let's say you help him increase his productivity to 20 calls a day. In this example, salesperson B would also see a 100 percent increase in sales assuming his performance stays the same (close ratio of 1:10). Reference Tables 2 and 3 for a before and after snapshot.

Table 2. Before Sales Results

BEFORE

	Salesperson A	Salesperson B
Number of calls per day (productivity)	20	10
Close ratio (performance)	1:20	1:10
Total sales per day	1	1

Table 3. After Sales Results

AFTER

	Salesperson A	Salesperson B
Number of calls per day (productivity)	20	20
Close ratio (performance)	1:10	1:10
Total sales per day	2	2
Percentage increase in sales	100%	100%

In this hypothetical example, we focused *only* on performance (close ratio) for salesperson A and *only* on productivity (number of calls) for salesperson B to illustrate the difference between performance and productivity. To get a 100 percent increase in overall team sales requires a different focus for each sales rep. If this were a real sales team, we would obviously want to see it focus on both performance *and* productivity for *all* its sales reps—just as the sales team did that went from averaging 17 to 34 sales that we discussed in Chapter 1.

Although we used a sales example to make this point, you can apply the same approach to logistics, programming, HR, healthcare, and many other job functions. No matter what type of industry or job position we are talking about, this kind of transformation does not come about from wishful thinking; it is the development of the mindset and a skillset that directly impacts both performance and productivity.

Here's another performance and productivity analogy: imagine two archers who have a target set up 20 feet away. Both archers get three arrows to shoot as part of a competition. The objective is to hit the bullseye. The further away the arrows land from the bullseye, the fewer points the archers earn. Imagine that the first archer shoots three arrows and hits the target but misses the bullseye (reference Figure 1).

Although the archer does score a handful of points for hitting the target, they did not hit the bullseye. In other words, the archer shot all three arrows (productivity) but was not hitting the mark (performance). Productivity was high, but the performance was low.

Now, imagine the second archer takes a slow deep breath, checks the notch of the arrow, and shoots an arrow that hits the bullseye (reference Figure 2). But this archer then chooses not to shoot the other two arrows.

Although the second archer was accurate with the arrow—they hit the bullseye—the points were still limited because the second archer only shot one arrow rather than three. Wouldn't it be remarkable if the second archer could add two more arrows to the bullseye in the same output as the first archer? In other words, this archer performed at a high level, but missed out on additional points by not shooting more arrows (productivity)—performance was high, but productivity was low.

Figure 1. Productivity

Figure 2. Performance

The ideal scenario is an archer who is both high-performing and productive—four arrows (or more) on the bullseye! (See Figure 3.)

Figure 3. Performance and productivity

In this case, the high-performing archer hits the bullseye (performance) and repeats it multiple times (productivity); both productivity and performance are high. These types of results are what any organization or team should strive for, *high-performance and productivity*.

This focus on vision, goals, and pre-week planning is why doing what matters most matters! With a focus on the big three, both performance and productivity increase and results can skyrocket—just as they did for both the hypothetical archer and sales reps.

Before moving on, let's use an example from outside the workplace to relay the same point. Imagine a person named Adam. Like many people, Adam's been so busy with his career, family, and everything else that his focus on his own health and exercise has not been what it could be. So, he has decided, this is the year!

In January, Adam sets a goal to run a half marathon by September 1st. If Adam wants to be successful, he needs to proactively focus on both performance and productivity. It is both the quantity *and* quality of exercise that makes the difference. For instance, it is not enough if Adam only works out once a week, even if it is a great workout. Likewise, if Adam works out several times a week, but the workouts are poor-quality, he won't be ready for the half marathon either. Adam must combine high-quality workouts (performance) with enough repetition (productivity) to achieve his goal.

As you can see, this focus on performance and productivity applies to your professional goals as well as your personal goals. Just like the salesperson example, Adam won't magically be ready for the half marathon without the right focus and preparation. He will likely fight the same battles that many fight during his preparation—procrastination, chasing the next shiny object, or being "too busy." In Adam's case, it is his vision, goals, and pre-week planning that will help him make time to train and prepare. For you, maybe it is not a half marathon; instead, perhaps you want to increase your focus on your health, mental and emotional well-being, job performance, or relationships.

We have observed that the best leaders want their team focused on high-impact activities and performing them as much as possible. In other words, we want our team members focused on what matters most and doing those things at a high level of output. Whether the team is working in manufacturing, sales, marketing, HR, or another function, the same thought process applies. For example, if you lead a group of technicians who service homes, you want those technicians to service as many homes as possible, delivering as close as they can to perfect service—productivity and performance. Isn't that a lot better than a technician who has a 20 percent return rate to fix problems that should have been addressed on their first visit?

Everything we have just talked about may seem obvious, but it is amazing how, in so many organizations, this area is ripe for improvement. When you look at your coworkers and others in your organization, what is your assessment of how they are doing when it comes to performance *and* productivity?

The focus on performance and productivity is a great starting point for leaders who want to see a measurable impact on both the top and bottom line.

The fastest way to simply, yet powerfully, get people focused on both high-performance and productivity is to help them develop the big three, putting them in the 1 percent of people who have developed this skillset.

The Performance and Productivity Research

The idea of doing what matters most is directly tied to performance and productivity. When a leader focuses on performance and productivity in the *right* way, the leader can enact a significant impact on results, morale, turnover, attitude, and the well-being of their team members.

Many leaders recognize that time-management, performance, and productivity are areas worthy of attention and improvement. Yet, many have expressed a similar question, "How do we increase results effectively?" We understand time is precious, and you do not want to waste your resources on something that does not work or only has limited benefits. The intent in collecting the data in our research was to identify what would truly have an impact on both performance and productivity.

When we started this research, the statistics related to performance and productivity were eye-opening. Take a look at just a few of these statistics and think about how they might relate to you and your organization:

- 34 percent of US workers are actively engaged (as a side note, we realize other factors go into this statistic, but this is still an important data point when it comes to performance and productivity).[5]

- From a sample of 4,300 employees, 74 percent felt that they weren't achieving their full potential at work due to a lack of development opportunities.[6]

- 12 percent of employees have called in sick because of job stress.[7]

- 53 percent of employees give the minimum effort required—and will quickly leave for even a slightly better offer.[8]

- Once you've been derailed from a task by an interruption, it takes an average of 23 minutes to get back on track.[9]

- The typical business professional sends and receives 122 emails daily.[10]

- When just one or two team members make even a small fumble (missed deadlines, forgotten tasks, etc.), team productivity declines by an average of 24 percent.[11]

- Less than 10 percent of employees feel competent at setting clear goals and developing a plan.[12]

- Only 2 percent of executives, managers, and employees have a written personal vision.

- 68 percent of people feel their number one challenge is how to prioritize their time.

- 80 percent of people do not have a process to prioritize their time and do what matters most.

- 84 percent of people feel like they would be significantly more productive if they had a process to help them prioritize their time.

- More than 74 percent of employees feel they don't devote enough time to their physical, mental, and emotional health.[13]

- Average employee productivity is between 45 and 50 percent.[14]

Of course, all these numbers are just a sampling of the revealing research into performance and productivity.

We also found the leading causes of lost productivity include procrastination, distraction, unimportant meetings, lack of direction, lack of initiative, feeling overwhelmed, and wasted time on electronic media. The combination of any two or all of these factors can have a significant overall impact on productivity and results.

In our experience, by focusing on performance and productivity, leaders have one of the most significant opportunities to see a real increase in results.

The Do What Matters Most Matrix

In Chapter 1, we commented that success requires both a mindset *and* a skillset. Leaders need to believe that anyone can change or improve when equipped with the right mindset and skillset.

Let's take Jill's story as an example. She is part of an organization that has about 500 employees. She has been with the company for nearly 10 years, and if you were to look through her past performance evaluations, you would see that up until relatively recently, she was considered a mediocre team member. She was moderately productive but certainly not even close to being considered a high performer. She would eventually get the assigned tasks done, and her work would often contain a handful of mistakes that needed correcting. Her work was considered average at best.

Two years ago, however, Jill learned about the big three. She developed her personal vision, identified her roles and goals for the year, and committed to do pre-week planning each week. With this shift in mindset and a new skillset, she vaulted to the top 10 percent of peers within her organization.

Three months after she had started applying this skillset, her direct supervisor wrote us an email. He was astonished by Jill's transformation. He wrote that she transformed into an entirely new team member. She went from being average to being one of the best team members in the entire division. As a result of her vision, goals, and pre-week planning, these are some of the transformations Jill experienced:

- She exercised for 40 minutes during her lunch break.
- She devoted the remaining 15 to 20 minutes of her lunch break to reading or listening to a book that would help her improve her life and workplace.
- She began meditating several times a week to help with her anxiety.
- Her office productivity went up by more than 50 percent on tasks accomplished due to pre-week planning.
- She became a solution finder and a contributor to the team.

- She told her supervisor that at home she was using her time to engage in meaningful activities with her husband and kids.

- She lost 40 pounds in just 90 days (which was a big deal to her)!

There are thousands of Jill stories out there that come from the application of these simple, powerful habits! This type of increase in performance and productivity rarely happens by accident. Because of Jill's intentional planning and focus, her performance average went up, and every area of her life improved.

As they did for Jill, vision, goals, and the habit of pre-week planning will support you in making time for what matters most in *your* life.

• • • •

There is a matrix we use to put the focus on the right kind of activities; this matrix is a great starting point for identifying where a person or team currently is versus where they would ideally like to be (like Jill). This matrix was originally called the *Eisenhower Matrix*.

The Eisenhower Matrix was named for and created by Dwight D. Eisenhower, 34th president of the United States, and one of only nine officers in the history of the United States Army to ever become a five-star general. He was the supreme allied commander who coordinated the invasion that became known as D-Day toward the end of WWII. History and modern business research have proven that his method of optimizing performance and productivity was exceptional. Over the years, various people have used Eisenhower's matrix with their own spin, but the essence has always been the same, and the credit goes to Eisenhower. We have taken the liberty of making a few adjustments to the Eisenhower Matrix; because of those adjustments we call it the Do What Matters Most matrix.

Let's take a closer look at the Do What Matters Most matrix in Figure 4 and see how it can support you and your team in focusing on what matters most. Although we describe each quadrant, see if you can identify where you (and your team) spend most of your time.

Figure 4. The Do What Matters Most matrix

	URGENT	**NOT URGENT**
IMPORTANT	**Q1** **DO IT!** High stress, high-priority **EXAMPLES** Crises, emergency meetings, client concerns, pressing problems, deadlines, fires, emergencies	**Q2** **FOCUS** Low stress, high-priority **EXAMPLES** Roles and goals, pre-week planning, weekly alignment meeting, relationship building, exercise, strategic planning, personal or team development
NOT IMPORTANT	**Q3** **MANAGE** Urgent, not important **EXAMPLES** Some email or mail, unnecessary meetings or reports, interruptions, unannounced calls or visits	**Q4** **ELIMINATE** Not urgent, not important **EXAMPLES** Some TV, surfing the internet, wasted time, mindless activities

Below is a brief description of each quadrant:

Q1—DO IT! This is the high-stress, high-priority quadrant. These activities demand your time because they are generally urgent *and* important. This quadrant is reactive by nature and describes the person or team that is often putting out fires. We will all be in Q1 periodically, but it should be the exception rather than the norm. If a person or team lives in this quadrant, there will likely be higher turnover, stress, anger, and frustration.

Some people thrive on the adrenaline of Q1. However, it is difficult to sustain high performance and productivity over an extended period because of the burnout that often accompanies Q1. Leaders need to be extra vigilant about minimizing their time in Q1, *especially* when they put other people on their teams in Q1 because of their own lack of planning. For example, the manager who is always dropping high-priority tasks on their team is likely to put their team into Q1 inadvertently, and it will have a big impact on performance and productivity.

Q2—FOCUS. This is the low-stress, high-priority quadrant. The activities are important but not urgent. This quadrant is proactive by nature and is where the majority of high performers live. This quadrant is all about scheduling your priorities to focus on what matters most while minimizing the amount of time spent in the other quadrants. An intentional focus on Q2 activities will make time for things like exercise, meditation, upcoming projects, relationships, planned rest or vacations, improving processes in the workplace, and so on. A person who does not focus or plan effectively will have many things in their life that should be Q2 activities that become Q1 activities. In other words, without sufficient focus and planning, something can become a crisis that should never have been one in the first place. We have all experienced the feelings that come with procrastination. For example, if we procrastinate and don't do our Q2 preparation, the closer a due date gets for something important, the more our stress increases.

People who have a vision and goals and who develop the habit of pre-week planning will primarily be in Q2. The big three are what help a person concentrate on what matters most and properly manage the other three quadrants while staying focused on high-performance and productivity.

Q3—MANAGE. This is the urgent, but not important quadrant. Activities in this quadrant require action but do not generally contribute to your goals or are not considered high-impact activities. People in this quadrant often focus on tasks such as sending emails and holding unnecessary meetings, and they fill up the time by asking for things like unnecessary reports. The idea is to manage the emails, phone calls, text messages, reports, or projects by what quadrant they apply to. Move an item to Quadrant 1 or 2, discard the item, skip the email, or automate the task. A good manager wants to get in and out of Quadrant 3 as soon as possible. Determine whether it is important or not!

Q4—ELIMINATE. This is the not urgent and not important quadrant. Q4 includes any activities that waste your time, do not support your vision, or are not helping you in any way. Without intentional planning, a lot of activities during the day end up being a waste of time, and this is one of the reasons why productivity and performance suffer.

You likely know someone who spends the majority of their time in each of these quadrants. Where do you spend most of your time? Where do you think your coworkers spend their time? Maybe you know the person who seems to love the thrill of the firefight, and it seems like they create chaos and fires so that they can put them out. That is a person who is continually reacting to the fire of the day and lives in Q1. Maybe you know the person who seems to skate by, doing the minimal amount of work required for their job, that is a Q3 or Q4 person, and it is often frustrating to work with them.

Our research indicates that the optimal high-performance and productivity balance for a person or team is to spend 20 to 25 percent of their time doing Q1 activities, 60 to 70 percent of their time focusing on Q2 activities, 5 to 15 percent of their time managing Q3 activities, and less than 5 percent in Q4 activities. These numbers vary somewhat by industry but hold true in most.

That same research shows that individuals and organizations that struggle and are far less productive spend 40 to 50 percent of their time in Q1, 15 to 20 percent of their time in Q2, 30 to 40 percent of their time in Q3, and 10 to 15 percent in Q4.

Two powerful questions to consider are these: What is the impact on you and others of being in each of these quadrants? What are the feelings you and others experience in each quadrant? Your answer to these questions will affect both your desire to focus on a specific quadrant and the results that come from that focus. Both knowledge and emotion are big motivators!

• • • •

For years, Jill hovered between Q3 and Q4, which is why her supervisor categorized her as a mediocre employee. When she effectively applied the new skillset of the big three, her efforts and activities moved to Q2. Jill's shift in focus transformed her life, and she discovered an entirely new world. Her life improved, her productivity and performance increased, and she became one of the top employees in the entire division.

This type of transformation—the Q2 focus—happens because a person sees through the lens of an inspiring personal vision, clear roles and goals, and pre-week planning. This skillset gives a person a clear lens to determine what is most important or urgent.

We heard from Jill about a year after she started working on the big three, and she enthusiastically said, "This past year has been the best year of my life!" Why? Because she put in the effort to determine what mattered most to her (Q2) and then focused on those things.

You also might remember Amy from the introduction. It was her focus on the big three that helped her move to Q2 and transform her life. Before her transformation, without realizing it, she had been spending way too much time, more than 50 percent of her day, in Q1 and Q3. But instead of living in Q1 or Q3, she learned how to prioritize what mattered most and when to *do* the Q1 items. After just one month of implementing these new habits, she was finally giving her husband and special-needs daughter the time they deserved. Her supervisor told Amy that she had never seen her so productive and happy. Amy was leading her team with renewed vigor and a significantly improved attitude. Most importantly, Amy was also prioritizing her own well-being!

When Amy was spending half her time in Q1 and Q3, she was continually reacting to the fire of the day and chasing meaningless targets—each day she was effectively "winging it." Armed with a new mindset and skillset, she moved into Q2 and took control of her life by doing what mattered most. As a result, her performance and productivity increased, her stress decreased, she was a better leader to her team, and she had a renewed energy and outlook on life. Q1 emergencies still cropped up each week, but Amy was in a much better position to handle them and, because of her focus and planning, they became the exception rather than the norm.

Many people reading this can probably relate to Jill or Amy in one way or another. Most people have good intentions floating around in the back of their minds, and they want to do what matters most. Whether it is increasing productivity at work, nurturing meaningful relationships, maintaining their health, or finding a purpose, people want to improve these important areas of their lives. For most, it is just a matter of learning a process that helps them schedule their priorities rather than prioritize their schedule. It is developing the ability to move past all the reactionary sticky notes and to-do lists to find the peace and confidence to *do what matters most* (Q2)!

Q2 Priorities

We want to share one final analogy to illustrate how important it is to think in terms of what matters most and Q2 (and periodically Q1).

Imagine a classroom full of students with two large, empty glass aquariums at the front. The teacher is standing, facing the students, behind the two aquariums. The teacher pours a box full of ping pong balls into the first aquarium until the balls are level with the top.

The teacher then asks the students, "Is the aquarium full?" The response, "Yes!"

Then, without saying a word, the teacher takes out a box of small rocks and dumps those into the aquarium. The rocks find the small seams and holes between the ping pong balls until they are also level with the top of the aquarium. The teacher again asks, "Is the aquarium full now?" The students respond hesitantly, "Yes?"

Again, without saying a word, the teacher takes out another box filled with fine grains of sand and dumps it in the aquarium. Like the rocks, the sand filters through any little opening it can find until it reached the brim of the aquarium. The teacher then asks the class for a third time, "Is the aquarium full?" The not-so-confident response is, "Maybe?"

Finally, the teacher pulls out a large pitcher of water and dumps the water into the same aquarium. The water fills in any final gaps and ultimately reaches the rim. With a smile on her face, the teacher again asks, "Is this aquarium full?" The students seem more confident now and yell, "Yes!" This time the students are correct—reference Figure 5.

Figure 5. The full aquarium

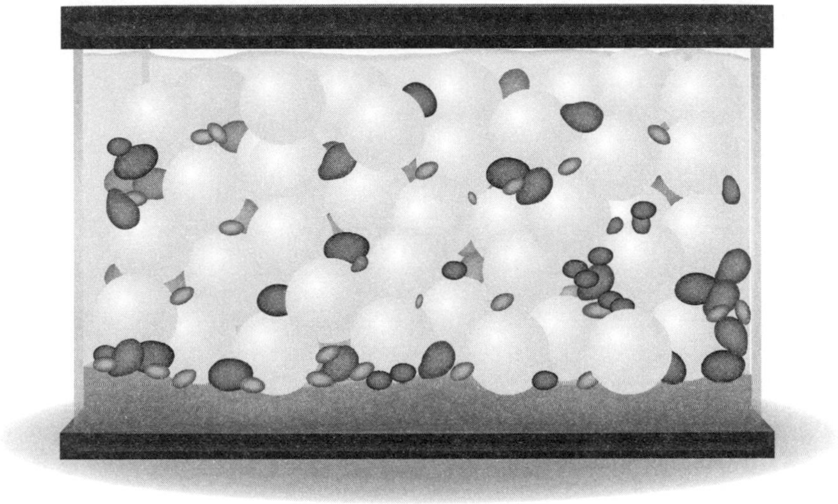

The teacher then moves over to the other aquarium and pulls out a large container of water. The teacher dumps the water into the aquarium and fills it right to the brim. The teacher then asks the students, "Is this aquarium full?" The perplexed students are not sure how to respond, and the teacher hears some saying "Yes" and others saying "No."

The teacher then takes the same number of ping pong balls they initially put into the other aquarium and attempts to dump those into the aquarium full of water. As expected, the ping pong balls float and fall out of the aquarium. Obviously, with the aquarium full of water, there is no room for the ping pong balls—reference Figure 6.

Figure 6. The aquarium full of water

The point of the illustration is to demonstrate what happens in our lives if we let the small things crowd out the big things or, in other words, when we let the things that matter the least crowd out the things that matter most. When the ping pong balls were put in the aquarium first, there was still plenty of room for the small things (rocks, sand, and water). However, when the aquarium was filled with water first, there was no room for the ping pong balls. How many times do you see something similar in your life or the lives of your coworkers?

This analogy applies to both our personal and professional lives. It is why the big three are so important. They keep a person focused on what matters most (the ping pong balls) rather than on being crowded out by the things that matter least. These habits will move a person from any other quadrant and help them solidly stay in the high-performance and productivity area of Quadrant 2. Even when the random fire or urgent item comes up that requires them to step into Quadrant 1, it is only a temporary place. A person who has a vision and goals and understands the process of pre-week planning will be in a much stronger position to do what matters most and respond to any unexpected crisis or issue that may show up in Q1.

Time and Leadership

Time is the most precious resource we have. It is the great equalizer because it cannot be purchased and we all have the same amount of it. In today's culture, the words "I'm too busy" are all too familiar. In many cases, they seem to be used as an excuse not to focus on one's priorities. As a result, things that matter least (Q3 and Q4) seem to crowd out the activities that should matter most (Q1 and Q2). Another commonality is that people or teams get stuck in Q1, constantly reacting to the crisis of the day, never seeming to get ahead of the game. The implementation of the big three habits will move a person to Q2 and shift the focus back to what matters most.

As we mentioned earlier, over 80 percent of the executives we surveyed have never learned a process that prioritizes their time and allows them to do what matters most. So, if your coworkers or employees are not producing and performing at a high level, in many cases, it is not their fault. If they have never had the training or learned the skillset, how can you expect improved results? A person can only perform or produce to the level of their current mindset and skillset. If someone is expected to improve, then there needs to be a change in mindset and/or skillset; otherwise, they are expected to do something they have never learned how to do. In the earlier examples of salesperson A and salesperson B, their increase in performance and productivity only came as a result of a new skillset and mindset.

To illustrate this point, we were working with a Division I football coach, and he said, "I have several players who have great talent but bad attitudes. They constantly complain and focus on the negative. It is like they are a cancer to the team. What should I do with them?" Our initial response was to ask him, "Have you done everything you can, as their leader, to give those players the right training? In other words, you need to ask yourself whether you have given them the training to develop the right mindset and skillset."

We then went on to explain that if the answer is *yes*, then you either find a different position for those players or get them off the team as fast as you can. If the answer is *no*, and you have not given them the mindset and skillset training, then that is a leadership issue that comes back to you and the coaching staff—in other words these players need the training. Without the right training, they will keep doing what they have always done. Having said that, if they have been trained with the right tools or skills and still do not change, then that is on them.

What we were saying to that coach applies to all of us, whether we are talking about coworkers, team members, or even our own family. Most people have not learned a skillset to prioritize their time and move to Quadrant 2. They are only doing what they have learned up to this point in their lives, and if the expectation is that they improve, they need a new skillset to help them. Before a person can be expected to perform at a higher level, they need to learn the processes and tools that will help them lead their lives and make a move to Quadrant 2!

Wrap Up

When you apply the Q2 habits of vision, roles and goals, and pre-week planning, they will improve every area of your life. This focus on both your personal and professional lives is what raises your *performance average.* For example, we found that a person who has a significant personal issue in their life will be about 40 percent less productive at work. By reverse logic, a person who has a balance of success stories will be 40 percent more productive in the workplace. Likewise, according to our research, a person who exercises and eats well will often be at least 15 percent more productive than someone who does not.

The combination of these habits will help you make time where you did not know it existed. You will feel the power that comes with a sense of direction and purpose. Task saturation and stress will both decrease while performance and productivity increase. You will take care of your physical and mental health as well as devote more quality time to the important people in your life. In short, we are confident that the application of these three habits will support your journey to having one of the best years of your life. We can confidently make that statement because we have seen it happen in our own lives, the lives of people like Amy and Jill, and the lives of thousands of others.

It is the combination of these three habits that shift a person's focus to Q2 and raises their performance average. When a person applies the habits, it is like the archer who shoots more arrows and hits the bullseye. It is focusing on the ping pong balls, or the essential items, rather than focusing on the small things (pebbles and water).

These three habits work in unison. It is not one without the others. They are designed to take a person from the 30,000-foot view of their life (the vision) down to where the rubber meets the road in the daily and weekly actions (pre-week planning). That is why it is critical to read the next six chapters carefully. These chapters are paired; in the first we introduce each habit, and then, in the subsequent chapter, we explain how to work it into your life.

To get started, let's begin with the power of a personal, written vision!

REFLECTION QUESTIONS FOR THIS CHAPTER:

1. What quadrant(s) do you spend most of your time in right now? Why?

2. How does each quadrant feel? How would it feel for you to be primarily in Q2?

3. How can you help your team and organization maximize effectiveness by having a strong focus on Q2 and efficiently handling Q1s?

4. What is one area of your personal *and* professional life where you feel you could improve performance and productivity?

3

The Power of a Personal Vision

What do people like the Wright brothers, Martin Luther King Jr., Amelia Earhart, Hellen Keller, George Washington, Rosa Parks, Gandhi, Harriet Tubman, and so many others have in common? Although none of them was perfect, the one common thread that binds them all together is they had a clear personal vision that was meaningful to them.

When you read some of these names, you may think that you will never have that kind of impact on the world. It is important to understand that your personal vision does not have to change the world; it just has to change *your* world! Whether you are the CEO, a frontline team member, a stay-at-home parent, or a student, you can develop a written, personal vision that is meaningful to you.

Imagine how great it would feel to have a sense of purpose, clarity, and direction. To wake up in the morning excited to face the day. High-performing employees and great leaders have such a vision. It is what provides fuel to the fire of their lives.

To use the metaphor of a seed, we believe that your personal vision is the seed of your legacy. Imagine the massive trees that grow in the redwood forest. They can be up to 240 feet high and up to 15 feet in diameter, and every one of those giant trees started as a small seed. Likewise, most great accomplishments start with the seed of an idea.

You have likely heard about creating a personal vision many times throughout your life. However, in our research, we have found that it is talked about a lot more than it is done. In fact, as we shared earlier, only 2 percent of the people we surveyed had a written personal vision. In this chapter and the next, we want to help you plant your seed and develop a compelling written vision that is meaningful to you.

When it comes to performance and productivity, one of the most important things a person can do is to articulate their vision. Imagine, from a managerial perspective, how great it would be to have a team of people, where each member is clear on their direction and purpose; is engaged; has a desire and passion for being there; and has a personal vision that aligns with the team and organization. The process of developing a personal vision can be transformative both for the person and for the entire team.

The unique approach to developing your vision shared in this chapter and the next will help you establish a well-rounded vision that will impact *all* aspects of your life!

The Wright Brothers

Before we get started on your personal vision, let us examine the Wright brothers to see what impact their vision had in changing the course of history. Their vision gave them the direction, motivation, and encouragement to successfully design and fly the first aircraft—a feat that changed the world.

So, what was their vision? To successfully build and develop a flying machine!

It is interesting to see how this vision came about. The Wright brothers first conceived the idea that man could fly in August of 1896. Keep in mind that Orville and Wilbur did not even understand the principles of flight at this point. That August day was important because once they conceived the thought—the seed of the idea—it was the beginning of what ultimately became a powerful vision. It was their vision that guided their behavior, focus, learning, and time. And it was this vision, coupled with their background and ingenuity, that made modern flight a reality.

Only after they conceived the *vision* to fly did they work on *how* to fly—first the vision, then the reality. It is the same with us; we first need to develop the vision, then we can work on the how-to. The following is a brief background of the Wright brothers and how their vision led to manned flight.

Wilbur (1867–1912) and Orville Wright (1871–1948) were raised in Dayton, Ohio. One day, their father brought home a small toy helicopter made of wood. It had two rubber bands that, when twisted, turned a small propeller. Wilbur and Orville played with it until it broke; then they made new copies of the toy themselves. They began to make additional toy helicopters and sell them to their friends. Thus, their newfound curiosity and innovation led them into the world of flight.

Years later, the Wright brothers opened their first bicycle shop. Initially, they sold and repaired bicycles. They would replace spokes, fix broken chains, and sell accessories. Then in 1896, they began to build their own brand of bicycles. All of their bicycle experience helped them in their investigations of flight. They used the technology they learned from their bicycle business in their airplanes: chains, sprockets, spoke wires, ball bearings, and wheel hubs. Their thoughts on balancing and controlling their aircraft were also rooted in their experience as cyclists.

In 1900, they built their first machine designed to carry a pilot and chose Kitty Hawk, NC, as a suitable testing ground. With its strong, steady winds, open areas, and tall sand dunes, it was perfect for their experiments. When their initial aircraft design produced less lift than expected, the Wright brothers flew it as a kite and gathered more information that would enable them to design improved machines. They needed more practice, so they developed what they called a "wind tunnel" to help them simulate the conditions of flight while they worked to improve the design.

In 1902, using the wind tunnel, they discovered that to solve the control problems, they needed to add a rudder (see Figure 7). Discovering the importance of a rudder was one of the breakthroughs they needed to be able to fly successfully.

Figure 7. A diagram of the Wright Flyer

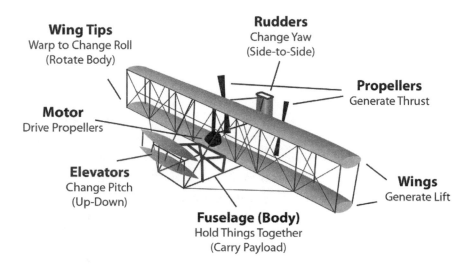

At Kill Devil Hills, on December 17, 1903, at 10:35 a.m., the Wright Flyer took off under its own power with Orville as the pilot (see Figure 8). It flew for 12 seconds and went about 100 feet. Orville and Wilbur took turns making three more flights that morning. Wilbur was at the controls for the fourth and longest flight, traveling about 800 feet in 59 seconds. The Wright 1903 Flyer became the first powered, heavier-than-air machine to achieve controlled, sustained flight with a pilot aboard. Today, this amazing flying invention can be seen at the National Air and Space Museum in Washington, DC.

In subsequent years, the Wright brothers continued to make modifications and improvements, until they got to the point where they could repeatedly bank, turn, circle, and do figure eights with their flyers. On two occasions, their flights exceeded half an hour. Wilbur and Orville Wright, brilliant self-trained engineers, had overcome complex technical problems that had barred the way to mechanical flight for centuries.[15]

Imagine the power of that single vision and the impact it had on the next century!

Figure 8. First flight[16]

Naysayers likely told the brothers that what they were doing could not be done. They had hundreds of setbacks, and like most innovators, they were likely tempted to quit at different points on their journey. But their vision was clear, and it provided them with a well of motivation and direction.

It was the combination of their mindset and skillset that helped them turn the impossible into the possible.

Although we used the Wright brothers to illustrate the power of a vision, we will repeat this: your vision does not need to change *the* world, it just needs to change *your* world!

The Influence of a Personal Vision

Nearly everyone agrees that it is important to align a team and an organization with a clear vision. Well, if it is critical for a team to be aligned with a vision, isn't it also important for each of us to have a vision that creates alignment in our personal and professional lives?

In the Wright brothers example, you saw something that changed the world; now let's use a couple of personal examples to illustrate how a personal vision can also change *your* world.

• • • •

We had just finished leading a two-day conference in Johannesburg, South Africa. At the time, one of the participants, named Jeff (who has since become a close friend), explained that he was leading an organization of approximately 2,000 employees. It was evident to us from his demeanor and the way he talked that he genuinely cared about his employees and the success of his organization.

During the conference, it became apparent that Jeff had endured several personal trials during the prior year and that they had tested him to the core. He shared that he was at a real low point in his personal life and that the things he was dealing with personally were also taking a significant toll on his ability to lead his company effectively.

After the conference was over, people left, except Jeff. While we were taking down the equipment, Jeff walked up behind us and placed a pack of cigarettes on a nearby chair. We turned around, saw Jeff standing there with moist eyes, and asked him what was going on. Jeff responded, "For years I have wanted to stop smoking cigarettes. I have smoked more than a pack a day, sometimes two, for a long time. Finally, it was when I developed my vision that I realized cigarettes were no longer a part of my future. This pack [pointing to the partially empty pack of cigarettes] is the last pack of cigarettes I will ever use. My vision has changed!" He had discovered that his internal *why* was now big enough to take on the challenge that had eluded him for years. We embraced in a big hug and congratulated him on his newfound vision and motivation.

Jeff related that he had thought about quitting smoking for years. The same exercise you will use in the next chapter to develop a personal written vision is the one that finally gave Jeff the internal drive to make a change. Implementing the big three became a turning point in Jeff's life. It was his focus on his vision, his roles and goals, and his pre-week planning that turned him around and helped him reconnect with a purpose. When you go through the same process of developing your vision, you will likely feel a similar internal desire for improvement.

What is powerful about a vision is that when we have one, we intuitively know when our life is either in alignment or out of alignment with this vision. When our lives are out of alignment with our vision, it is our responsibility to get back into alignment—just like Jeff did on that day in Johannesburg.

• • • •

In a more personal example, we will share how a personal vision changed Rob's life when he was 16 years old, shortly after his junior year in high school. That year was tough for him while he was trying to figure out life; he felt lost and confused. His confidence was low, he did not have any direction, and he certainly was not motivated. But everything changed on a warm July evening. It happened when he and his brother Steven attended the Stadium of Fire in Provo, Utah—one of the largest Independence Day celebrations anywhere in the United States.

The festivities kicked off with a fantastic fly-by of four F-16 fighter jets, which is always a great experience. When the jets flew by, everyone felt the roar of the engines reverberate through their bodies. Rob and his brother watched in awe while the jets flew over in perfect formation. Rob and Steven looked at each other and agreed, "Someday we're going to fly those jets over this stadium."

That warm July evening, focus and clarity came into Rob's life—the seed was planted, and the beginning of his vision was born!

From that point forward, Rob committed to act on that vision to become a fighter pilot. A wayward and lost teenager now had a laser-like focus, and everything changed in his life. He went to work on the plan to achieve his vision. He knew he would need to graduate from high school, do well at the university level, and compete with a lot of cadets for a coveted pilot slot. At 17 years old, after the required flight lessons, he earned his pilot's license, which further fueled his internal flame to become a fighter pilot.

Many years later, both Rob and Steven became F-16 pilots in the United States Air Force. After years of preparation and hard work, they were much closer to making their vision from the Stadium of Fire a reality.

Fifteen years after sitting in the stadium as young teenagers, Rob and Steven applied to the Pentagon for approval to do the fly-by for the Stadium of Fire. Fortunately, the Pentagon approved their request. Although each of them had experienced some pretty amazing things during their fighter pilot careers, they knew this fly-by would be the proverbial icing on the cake.

On July 4, 2007, their vision became a reality. Rob and Steven, in a four-ship formation, opened the celebration and performed the fly-by for the Stadium of Fire. In Figure 9, you can see a picture from Rob's jet looking at Steven's jet on the far side of the formation.

Figure 9. Flying in formation

After they flew over the stadium, the ground controller came over the radio and said, "Nice fly-by. Perfect timing. Congratulations, Shallenbergers!" The hair on both of their arms stood up, and both felt tears in their eyes. It was a special moment for everyone involved. Their entire family was in the stadium watching, many also with tears streaming down their cheeks.

It was the seed of their personal vision that was planted when Rob was 16 years old that led to this memorable experience. At 15 years to the day, his vision became a reality!

No matter what your vision is, once you have it, it becomes the spark that ignites the fire inside. Once you have your vision, you are able to develop your roles and goals and consistently do pre-week planning to work toward accomplishing that vision.

Create the Mental Reality Before the Physical Reality

One of the biggest challenges when we develop a vision is getting past the hurdle between our ears—our mindset. One of the most important things you can do in the process of developing your vision is let the creative ideas flow and not worry about all the constraints and roadblocks of what is and is not possible.

Let's equate the importance of the mindset to designing and building your dream home. Imagine in your mind's eye the look and feel of your dream home. Envision yourself driving up to your finished home, walking to the front door, and entering the home. Imagine looking in the main room and admiring every feature. In your dream home, you have had no constraints. You have been able to build whatever you want. Imagine looking at the woodwork, the landscaping, the beautiful kitchen, and the living room. What do you see?

Now, let's backtrack and think about what you need to build this home. At a minimum, you need money, property, and a plan (like the one you might see in Figure 10).

Figure 10. Dream home schematic

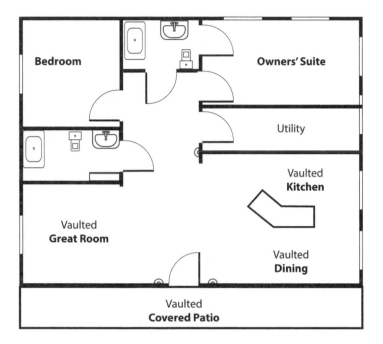

Would you build your home without a blueprint or plan? Of course not! Without a solid plan, the home may not meet code, you may have costly overruns and miscommunicate with contractors, and undoubtedly, the home would turn out differently than you had envisioned.

When you have a plan, you can see everything beforehand. You can see the result in your mind's eye before the house is even built. You can go over the plans with your partner and family to be sure everyone agrees. And, once you begin construction, the plan serves as a communication tool to be sure everyone is aligned.

If you only had one shot at building your dream home, you would be meticulous about your plans. Likewise, we only get one shot at life, so how important is it to have a solid plan for it?

When building your dream home, you use your imagination to create the thought, or mental picture, of the home. Then, you get to work on actually building and constructing it.

Your personal vision is about creating the mental reality before the physical reality. Once you dream it, then you can achieve it. Once you have it clear in your mind's eye, then you become intently focused on it. The journey of life gets exciting when you can get up in the morning and know what your best looks like because you have seen it in your mind's eye. Your personal vision will add direction, texture, light, color, imagination, music, richness, and amazement to your life.

A Clear Vision Can Transform Your Life

A vision has preceded almost every great accomplishment throughout history. Think of these famous visions:

- John F. Kennedy—Put a man on the moon.
- Rosa Parks—Equality for all.
- Elon Musk—Put people back into space, colonize the moon, go to Mars.
- Amelia Earhart—Be the first woman to fly alone across the Atlantic.
- Bill Gates—Have a computer in every home.

Each one of these influential leaders were guided by their vision. Successful leadership is about leading a life by *design* rather than living a life by *default*!

From the managerial perspective, leadership is about bringing out the best in others. One of the best ways to lead your life, and bring out the best in your team, is to first have your own inspiring personal vision and then help each person on your team develop theirs.

In his legacy book *Good to Great*, Jim Collins talks about getting your people in the right seats on the bus.[17] Think about how much easier it is to get a person in the right seat when you, as the leader, understand their talents, strengths, and *especially* their vision. In most cases, a team member whose personal vision is in alignment with the team and organization is a better contributor and a higher performer.

Likewise, focusing on teams is what successful executives and leaders do. Imagine the power of a team in which each person has a written personal vision that inspires them and brings out their best. Even better is a team made up of people who have inspiring personal visions, who develop their roles and goals, and who consistently do pre-week planning. The odds are that this will be a high-performing team because its members are well-versed on high-performance habits!

To take it a step further, if you are a parent, imagine helping your children develop a written vision that is meaningful to them. Leadership in the home is just as important, if not more important, than leadership in the workplace.

From the parenting perspective, Steve and his wife Roxanne tried to provide their children with opportunities that allowed them to see and learn new things. Steve and Roxanne believed that one of the serendipitous things in life is that in the right moment, providence would move on their behalf, and their children would each have a moment to capture a vision or dream that would have a profound influence on each of their lives.

Remember how Rob and Steven were inspired while sitting in the Stadium of Fire watching the F-16 fly-by? Another example of this type of inspiration resulted from when Steve took his children to the county and state political conventions when they were young. One of his sons, David, still has photos that he took with elected officials when he was just 12 years old. David was so impressed with public service that 30 years later, he got involved with politics at the state level. He, too, captured a vision about becoming a public servant, and years later, he is acting on that vision.

Similar things happened with Steve's other children. Each one was shown ideas, seized an inspiration, identified a course of action aligned with their strengths, and formed a personal vision that had a deep impact on each of their lives. Of course, none of the children is perfect, but what came from their personal visions has changed their lives as well as the lives of many others.

In one final example of leadership in the home, as part of her vision, Roxanne (in the role of mother) wanted each of her children to learn how to play the piano. Steve was excited about this vision and fully supported her efforts to find a teacher and, later, to shuttle the children to their many lessons and to help them practice and learn to play. As a result of her vision and hard work, all six of Steve and Roxanne's children learned to play the piano. This tradition has continued with Steve and Roxanne's grandchildren, who are all currently playing or learning how to play the piano. This type of legacy did not happen by accident. It was Roxanne's vision, leadership, motivation, and encouragement that created it.

Taking someone's native interests, helping them plant the seeds, and encouraging them to cultivate those seeds is one of the greatest gifts you can give them—whether you are in the workplace or in the home, this is the essence of leadership!

Wrap Up

The famous lecturer and poet Ralph Waldo Emerson wisely said, "What lies behind you and what lies in front of you, pales in comparison to what lies inside of you." A personal vision is exponentially more powerful when it is founded on character and correct principles. Each of our personal visions is about more than the destination; it is also about who we will become in the journey toward the destination.

Your personal vision, which lies inside of you, will change your world and all those around you as it deeply blesses and influences your life for good.

Developing a written personal vision is the first of the big three habits that are such strong predictors of high productivity and success. Once finished, your vision will become a wellspring of motivation and serve as your internal compass. It will become the guide for your roles and goals, and then later, for your pre-week planning.

Now, let's get started on how to develop *your* personal vision!

REFLECTION QUESTIONS FOR THIS CHAPTER:

1. How would having a guiding personal vision affect your life?

2. What area of your life would be most affected by having more direction and focus?

3. How could you help your coworkers or team members (or family) develop their personal vision? What would the impact be?

4

How to Develop a Personal Vision

Now it is time to start on your personal vision. To set the right expectations, we must clarify that this is not something you do in just a few minutes. It will take a lot of thought, effort, and emotion on your part. You will be most effective when you use a pen and paper so that you can physically write. The other alternative is to have a tablet you can write on, but the point is that you actually write. The act of writing unlocks a part of your brain that otherwise stays dormant—strangely, typing alone does not unlock it. If you would like some help getting started, a free vision template is available from BYBgoals.com.

So, whether you are using a blank piece of paper, our template, or a tablet, let's get started.

Follow these three steps to develop a compelling personal vision.

Step 1. Fire Up Your Imagination!

Just as you imagined your dream home in the last chapter, you first need to identify what you want your life to look like so that you can work on making it a reality. Step 1 is about creating your mental reality so you can start working toward making that your physical reality.

Four questions will help fire up your imagination so that you can start thinking about what matters most to you and what the best version of you looks like. These questions will help you get your creative ideas flowing *before* you start on your vision.

We constantly hear feedback from people who say that these four preliminary questions were vital to helping them think about what to include in their personal visions. Invest as much time as you need to answer these questions *fully*. It is easy to stay at the surface, but we invite you to go deeper. For some people, this might mean that you spend hours on just these four questions. At a minimum, you should spend no less than 15 minutes; if you spend less, you are likely shortchanging yourself.

Write these four questions on a tablet or a piece of paper and leave plenty of space for your answers:

A. In the next 10 to 20 years, what are some things you want to do and/or accomplish?

B. Think of any mentors or people who have inspired you (these can be people you know personally or people you know from history). What are the traits, characteristics, and qualities that you admire about each of these people?

C. What would you like to improve in your job, your home, or your community?

D. How do you hope others will look back and describe you 50 years from today, whether you are alive or not?

These four powerful questions help the mind think about what matters most. When you answer them, you will have started to design your home—or the mental reality of the best version of yourself—*before* starting on your vision.

Each question does its part to get the creative juices flowing. For example, question B asks you to think about mentors or influencers who have inspired you or who have had a positive impact on your life. Here are some answers to this question that we have seen in the past:

⊙ They brought out the best in me because they believed in me!

⊙ They had an uplifting and positive attitude.

- They had a sense of humor, knew how to laugh, and had fun.

- They sincerely listened to me when I needed a listening ear.

- They had hope and exercised great faith.

- They took responsibility for their actions and owned everything that happened to them.

- They treated me with kindness and respect.

Can you sense how powerful going through this process is just by reading a few of these answers? Question B often causes a person to say to themselves, "If those are the traits and qualities I admired in others, shouldn't those be the traits and qualities that I should be focusing on with myself?"

It is the reflective nature of each of the four questions that makes them important to think about *before* starting on your vision. Armed with your answers to these four questions, you will be ready to start on your actual vision.

Your vision is as much about *becoming* the ideal version of yourself as it is about accomplishing different things in life. It does not matter whether you are that person now or not; what is important is that you can articulate the type of person you want to become.

Step 2: Identify the Roles That Matter Most to You

We invite you to look at your life through the lens of the different roles that matter most to you. Throughout the day, you wear different hats based on where you are, what you are doing, and who you are with, right? A few examples of roles are personal (physical, mental, emotional, spiritual, and financial), parent, your job title, spouse or partner, coach, church member, friend, brother/sister, son/daughter, and so on.

When we think about roles in general, it is often easier to think just about our professional roles. Roles invite us to think about the other areas of our lives that are equally or even more important. Dividing your life into your most important roles helps you maintain balance and think about what you can accomplish or do in each area. Our focus on roles is what makes this book far more than just another one on business or leadership. This holistic approach to leading your life and focusing on your key roles supports the journey toward your best self.

Those of you who use the template found at BYBgoals.com can see how there are specific areas for your vision and goals within each role (see Figure 11). The rows labeled "Role" are places for you to write your most important roles. In Figure 12, you can see how the same process of dividing your life into various roles can be used in a different format. For now, we will focus on the vision within each role. Ignore the areas where it talks about goals; that will be the focus of Chapters 5 and 6.

Several times throughout the book, you will read that your *personal* role is the most important role because it is *you* taking care of *you* first—physically, mentally, emotionally/spiritually, and financially. A person can only share their light when they have light to share. Some people call this *self-care*. The bottom line is that it does not matter what you call it; the most important thing is that you are able to take care of yourself. When you do, you will be in a much better position to show up in your other roles.

People frequently ask what the right number of roles is for a person to have. Although there is no right or wrong answer to that question, the optimal number of roles is somewhere between five and seven. The number of roles you choose depends on your personality and your circumstances, which leaves you room to experiment with it. Remember, the whole point of roles is to create balance and focus on what matters most. You do not want to have too many roles because you only have so much time and bandwidth. Typically, the five-to-seven range is a good starting point for most people.

Now that you've considered some of your roles, write down the roles that matter most to you. Leave some space either below or next to your role so that you can write your vision in that space. For now, this is a draft, so do not worry about whether it is perfect or not. It is more important to simply start.

Figure 11. Visions and goals template

VISION AND GOALS FOR 202X		
Role: Personal (Physical, Mental, Emotional, Spiritual)		
Vision:		
Annual Goals:		
Role: Manager		
Vision:		
Annual Goals:	1	
	2	
	3	
	4	
Role: Parent		
Vision:		
Annual Goals:	1	
	2	
	3	
	4	
Role: Spouse or Partner		
Vision:		
Annual Goals:	1	
	2	
	3	
	4	

Figure 12. Visions and goals in a different format

My Personal Vision and Goals

"You will either lead a life by design or live a life by default!"

Role: Personal (Physical, Mental, Emotional, Spiritual) _____

Vision: _____

_____

_____

Goal(s):

   Physical: _____

               _____

   Mental: _____

               _____

   Emotional: _____

               _____

   Spiritual: _____

               _____

Role: _____

Vision: _____

_____

_____

Goal(s): _____

_____

_____

_____

_____

_____

Step 3: Write Your Vision for Each Role

Keep in mind your answers to the questions from Step 1. The reason you started with those questions was to get your mind thinking about what matters most to you. Now take some of your thoughts and ideas from those four thought-provoking questions and come up with your vision in each role.

Ask yourself, *What represents the best version of me in this role?* If you can aspire to be the best manager, parent, partner, sales rep, and so on, what will that look like by role? Again, first develop the mental reality of what your best looks like in each role so that you can then create the physical reality.

It is important to clarify the difference between a vision and goals. Think of the vision as the end destination—it is the absolute best version of you in that role, there is an emotional feel to it, and it guides your behavior and decision-making. The annual goals come later and become the specific milestones toward making your vision a reality. You'll find it much easier to come up with goals when you do so in the context of your vision. So, when you develop your vision, it does not need to be specific or measurable—that comes with the goals. The most important part of your vision is that it drives your behavior and creates alignment for your actions in that role.

When developing your vision, it is also essential that you use empowering words, such as *I am* or *I will*, rather than weaker words such as *someday, I hope*, or *to be*. Sense the difference between saying *I am a transformational leader who leads from the front* versus *I hope to be a better leader.* When you write your vision and goals, words matter!

If you are like us, then you appreciate examples because they often generate new ideas. Read the following examples of a personal vision by role, some personal and some professional, to get a better sense of what others have done:

Personal: I choose to live a balanced, healthy lifestyle, and I am in great physical shape. I maintain a high level of spirituality. I am financially free with no debt or financial obligations to anyone.

Spouse: I am a kind and caring spouse who always helps my husband/wife/partner feel like a 10! I am totally faithful in thought and action and constantly strive to compliment him/her, serve him/her, and be the husband/wife/partner of his/her dreams.

Friend: I surround myself with people who make me want to be a better person and who care about my success. I am a loyal, committed friend who is happy about the success of others. I create meaningful friendships and genuinely want to help, lift, and inspire when possible.

Parent: I am an example in thought and deed of what a kind and caring person looks like. I am the type of person I want my daughters/sons to marry. I am present with my children and continuously develop great memories with them. I invest the time and energy to help them see their potential, bring out their best, and make a difference in the world.

Sales Manager: I am a transformational leader who knows the stories of and invests in each team member. I set the tone so that each member of our team is inspired to give their best, and I am always focused on developing the mindset and skillset of each team member. I am the type of leader my team would still want to follow without the title!

Again, your vision is something that should create alignment and direction in a specific role. Intuitively, you will be able to look at your vision for each role and *know* whether you are in alignment with it. If so, great. If not, then it is your responsibility to take action to get your life in harmony with your vision.

Let us look at the spouse example in more detail. Rob's actual vision in the role of husband is, "I am a kind and caring husband who always helps Tonya feel like a 10. I am totally faithful in thought and action, and I constantly strive to compliment her, serve her, and be the husband of her dreams." Is that how it always goes in their relationship? Of course not. But Rob knows when his actions and words are out of alignment with that vision. When he has said or done something that is out of alignment, it is his responsibility to fix it and get back to the vision. That vision also drives his goals and weekly actions from pre-week planning. The whole point is that Rob's vision in the role of husband gives him a direction for his actions, and it is meaningful to him. That is what you should be able to say about your vision for each of your roles.

From a professional standpoint, wouldn't you want people on your team whose personal vision aligns with the team vision? Also, wouldn't you want people on your team whose personal vision aligns with what they are doing in their role? In our experience, if an employee's vision is out of alignment with the company vision or their role in the company, they will be a mediocre contributor or performer at best. Conversely, high performers and high achievers often find that their personal vision aligns with the company vision and their role. For this reason, everyone who goes through the Do What Matters Most training develops a vision for their professional role or job title.

You can imagine how aligning Elon Musk's vision is, as the founder of SpaceX, when he says, "We are going to colonize Mars." Elon may not be perfect, but his type of vision creates alignment and motivation. You can use the same thought process for each of your roles. In other words, you can develop a statement that aligns your behavior and actions to your best self in that role.

Here are a few more examples to help you generate additional ideas:

Personal: I am organized and in control of my time. I dive into new experiences with enthusiasm. I am always learning new and exciting things to keep me invigorated. I am grounded, focused, and deeply connected with my inner self.

Artist: I bring color and beauty to the world by creating paintings that spark joy in others. I learn skills and techniques that I then pass on to others. I spread joy through my paintings.

Student: I am a dedicated student who stays on top of homework and assignments. I continue to learn and grow through experiences in and out of the classroom.

And here are a few professional examples for various roles:

CEO: I lead by example and set the tone for our organization. I help my team stay aligned, focused, and motivated to be the industry leader in the lead generation software industry. I commit the time and resources necessary to develop the people, create a high-performance culture, and align the strategy.

Manager: I am a great manager who contributes to an outstanding team. I am a key player who always brings energy, enthusiasm, and a no-quit attitude to the team. I uplift the people that I work with and help them to become their best.

Sales Rep: I do whatever it takes to ethically and legally close the deal. I have a no-quit attitude when I'm smiling and dialing. I strive to serve the customer and over-deliver in everything I do. I'm a team player because we ultimately win as a team.

Independent Consultant: I am an empowered and collaborative leader who is passionate about working with others and helping them become successful leaders. I am a leader who drives diversity and believes in the power of diverse thinking for better decision-making.

Founder: I will build a 50+ million-dollar company and become a leader in the data center industry. I am a leader who leads with integrity, innovation, vision, and collaboration. I only surround myself with people who have a strong work ethic, contribute to the team, and strive to make our company a better place.

Warehouse Manager: Safety and quality are my highest priority. I am the type of leader who clearly communicates expectations and leads the safest, most efficient warehouse operations in the industry. I am engaged with my employees and continuously seek to improve our operations with perfection as the standard.

Hopefully, these examples will help you get started. It is vital to articulate your mental reality so that you can go to work creating the physical reality. Remember, the vision is the destination, and the goals (which come later) are the milestones to achieve the vision.

If you are in a position to do so, we invite you to pause here and invest whatever time is necessary to develop a draft of your vision. In the beginning, the most important thing is to simply write. Choose the roles that matter most to you, get your thoughts on paper, and get down the first draft of your vision. Then, you can sit back, read it, see how you feel, and decide whether it is your final vision or if you might need to make some adjustments.

After you get some initial thoughts on paper, or you get a rough draft of your written vision, you can run it through a litmus test. Once it passes the litmus test, odds are you have a great vision that creates alignment in your different roles.

The Litmus Test

A common question people ask after spending time working on their vision is *How do I know that I have finished?*

If you are like most people, the vision can be challenging because you are articulating the direction for who you are and what type of legacy you want to leave (by role). The ultimate litmus test is to ask yourself two simple questions: First, *Does my vision give me direction in each role?* Second, *Is it meaningful to me?* If you can answer yes to both of these questions, you are off to a great start!

Your vision does not need to capture everything; it just needs to capture *what matters most* to you. In addition to these two fundamental questions, here are some additional questions you can ask to ensure you covered what matters most in your vision. If you have already started writing down your vision, review your draft, and see if these introspective questions spark any additional ideas:

- *Does it describe my physical shape, fitness, and desired health?*
- *Does it describe how I manage my money and my desired finances?*
- *Does it describe my emotional strength?*
- *Does it describe how I respond to anger, stress, or chaos?*
- *Does it describe how I treat others (my spouse, children, and coworkers)?*
- *Does it describe how I learn and gain knowledge?*
- *Does it describe what kind of listener and communicator I am?*
- *Does it describe my outlook on life?*
- *Does it excite me?*

- *Does it describe my honesty and integrity—especially in the moment of choice?*
- *Does it describe how I take responsibility for my actions?*
- *Does it describe how I live in peace and balance?*
- *Does it describe what I do in the face of adversity, setbacks, and failure?*
- *Does it describe my faith?*
- *Does it describe my work ethic?*
- *Does it describe a state of being that moves me from where I am today?*

When you read your vision and agree that it gives you direction and is meaningful to you, you have a vision! When you can satisfactorily answer most of the questions in the preceding list, your vision has passed the litmus test, and you are in a very elite percentage of people. When you get to this point, you will have done what only 2 percent of people have done!

You should feel a sense of accomplishment, as well as a clear sense of purpose and direction. If you feel a little uncomfortable or even a little nervous, that is perfectly normal and is generally a good feeling. A personal vision can evoke a wide range of emotions because of how personal it is. The reason it is normal to feel both excitement and unease is that you are now like the elastic band example from Chapter 1—you are stretching yourself.

We invite you to go to your calendar right now and block off an hour or so to focus on developing and finalizing your vision. Ideally, you will do this within the next two weeks while it is fresh in your mind.

To help with accountability, you can write in the planned completion date here:

I will finish my personal vision by _____ (date).

Once you pass the litmus test and finalize your vision, we invite you to print it and put it in a place where you will see it often (at least weekly as part of your pre-week planning). For those of you who use the Becoming

Your Best planner, you can put it in the front of the planner under the Vision tab. The point is to keep it in front of you—otherwise, out of sight, out of mind.

For those who want to take it up a notch, we also invite you to memorize your vision by role. You will find that in the process of memorizing your vision, it will get deeply ingrained into your mind and heart. Imagine how great that will feel to have such a powerful internal compass!

Once you have finalized your vision, you can continue to build on this habit of staying centered on your vision. Some people find it helpful to create a *vision board*. A vision board is an excellent complement to your written vision. To create a vision board, simply put up pictures on a board that represent your vision. You can put your vision board in your closet, hallway, garage, office, or anywhere you will see it often.

Another way to build on your written vision is to develop a lifetime bucket list. Create a list of things you would like to do during your life. If you are in a relationship, both people can do this individually and then come together to compare lists and look for overlaps and make those a higher priority. Your bucket list can be part of your vision board or collocated with your written vision.

Both the vision board and bucket list are simple ways to continue building on your written vision. They give you added focus, direction, and energy.

However, the most important part of this process is to start developing your written personal vision by role. After all, the art is in the start. An old saying from an unknown author says, "You don't have to be great to start, but you have to start to be great." So, we invite you to start today.

Congratulations on getting to this point. The fact that you are here is a big deal!

The Life-Changing Impact of Your Personal Vision

It is interesting to hear stories from people about how their vision affected their focus and productivity, both in the workplace and in their personal lives. You might also like to see what others have written about their experiences while you consider your personal vision. Consider these testaments to the process:

"Obstacles only become visible when we lose sight of the goal." This quote is one of my favorites and embodies the importance of a personal vision to me. Not only is my vision important, but it also drives me from my very core. My personal vision gives my life purpose, direction, and focus. It is sometimes easy to lose sight of the vision, to forget "what you care about," or get lost in the monotony of life. When this happens, I notice that I am not as happy or fulfilled; however, as soon as I recognize this, I go back to my vision to see how my actions align with my vision. Many times, I've slipped up, and it is not aligned, but just that realization is powerful because I can make course corrections to get back in line. My vision has changed my life. It's what gives me drive and purpose.

—ANNE S. P.

I recite my vision from memory almost every morning, and it really fires me up and ignites a deep passion within me to truly bring out my best to meet the day's challenges. My vision still brings a smile to my face and gives me a sense of purpose and drive that leaves me feeling full at the end of each day when I reflect upon it.

—MICHAEL L.

For me, my personal vision allows me to have greater happiness and peace instead of sadness, pain, confusion, or despair. What I learned recently was, I could re-write my personal vision. This re-write still had the core elements from the previous vision. However, because of many experiences and challenges, the re-writing of my personal vision has brought more happiness and allowed me to take on additional tasks

*and challenges with greater calm and peace. Having a
personal and professional vision makes all the difference as
I continue my journey in life. My personal vision is the
foundation of doing what matters most each day.*

—JULIE R.

*Having a personal vision for the key roles in my life has had a
powerful impact because these statements help me remember
the kind of person I'm ultimately trying to become. Between
having a busy work schedule, a family of eight, and other
responsibilities, my weeks get hectic, and it is easy to lose focus.
But when I sit down and review my personal vision, for each
role, as part of my pre-week planning, it centers me again on
what I'm ultimately trying to accomplish in life. My personal
vision has had a huge impact on the outcome of my life because
it helps me to identify what really matters most. I strive to stay
focused on my vision, overcome obstacles, and to "lift" myself
and others to a better place as a result.*

—JEFF D.

*My personal vision is my guiding star, my compass,
and a standard from which I live my life. It is the measuring
rod for self-reflection and the foundation for all decisions.
My son even put it visually into a coat of arms that
reflects that vision . . . it is who I am.*

—DAVID C. P.

Wrap Up

Your personal vision is the seed of your legacy, your internal compass, and
ultimately, who you want to be and what you want to do in each role. In the

end, whatever story we tell ourselves, whatever mental picture we paint, that will become our reality!

James Allen, a British writer and poet, wisely said, "The vision that you glorify in your mind, the ideal that you enthrone in your heart, this you will build your life by, and this you will become."[18]

The act of writing your vision is a powerful process, so we invite you to put in the time and effort to start and finish it. It will be helpful if you actually block out time in your calendar to work on it until it is finished. For those of you in managerial roles, we then invite you to help your team start on their written personal visions. If you have children, and they are willing, you can help them develop their personal vision as well.

Once you have a draft of your personal vision, it is time to move on. The next two chapters focus on how to grow the seed and make your vision a reality through roles and goals!

REFLECTION QUESTIONS FOR THIS CHAPTER:

1. What was the experience of developing your personal vision like for you?

2. Who else do you know who would benefit from going through this process to develop a written personal vision (son/daughter, partner, team member)? Why would this process be helpful to them?

3. Where will you put your personal vision so that you can reference it each week as part of pre-week planning?

5

The Power of Roles and Goals

We have a friend who is the CEO of a well-known firm located in the Western United States. He is about 62 years old; we will call him Gary. Three years ago, he attended a three-hour workshop with his Young Presidents Organization (YPO) chapter.

He came up during the break (after starting on his vision and goals) to relate that during the past four years, he had felt like he had lost his edge. He was not making clear decisions as he had in the past. He also felt as if his passion for the business had all but disappeared. He had seriously considered turning over the entire business to his son.

After the first 90 minutes of the workshop, he excitedly told us that he had experienced a complete change in mindset. It was the act of starting on his vision and goals that reignited the flame he once had. He was excited and emotional when he commented, "I haven't felt this way for at least four years. I feel focused and see a clear path forward." We told him that what he was experiencing was just the beginning. We invited him to commit to finishing his vision and goals in the next two weeks. We also invited him to be consistent with the new habit of pre-week planning for the next three months and then call us with an update.

Three months later, Gary called us. He was excited and spoke very fast when he said, "The last three months have been some of the best of my life. I feel like I have my business edge back, my mind is clear and focused, and my personal life is as good as it has ever been. The last three months have been some of my most productive months in years!" He related that the first thing he had done was develop a vision that kindled his internal flame. He had realized that he was burned out and had lost his "why" for being in business. Developing his vision was the starting point to rediscover his "why."

During that call, Gary went on to explain that in conjunction with his vision, he had specifically written down one goal during the workshop that had a huge impact on him. During the conference, we had invited everyone to come up with a specific reading goal for the year, because, in our studies, we have found that reading and success are strongly correlated (either listening to an audiobook or actual reading is fine). Because of this correlation, we always invite people to come up with a specific reading goal. One of Gary's pivotal goals was to average reading at least one leadership book per month. It was interesting to hear him say that four years ago, when he started to lose his edge, he had also quit reading books. He used to be an avid reader, but for some reason, he had stopped. It was during the workshop that he realized he needed to start reading again.

He incorporated the Q2 activity of reading into his new goals, and doing so drove him to pick up the habit again. He commented on how that one goal was responsible for a massive improvement in his motivation, leadership, and decision-making. How much easier was it for Gary to get back on track after he identified what mattered most, developed his vision and goals, and then scheduled those priorities rather than succumbing to both task saturation and procrastination? He knew things like reading were important but, to use a pilot term, they had simply slipped out of his crosscheck.

We have heard stories similar to Gary's many times over the years—the truth is that we have all let important things slip out of our crosscheck at one time or another. The real power comes when people are willing and disciplined enough to finish their vision and their roles and goals and do pre-week planning consistently. Imagine the impact on performance and productivity when members of a team each have their own personal vision and well-written roles and goals for the year that keep them laser-focused!

Getting Started

The entire goal-setting process begins with gaining clarity on what matters most to you this year. We invite you to ask yourself these questions introspectively:

- *What would I like to accomplish this year?*
- *What are my targets this year, both personally and professionally?*
- *How do I specifically measure success in the different roles of my life?*
- *Are any of those objectives or thoughts written in the form of a goal? If so, how often do I look at them?*

These questions help people think about what matters most and where to direct their energy. Les Brown, author and motivational speaker, once said, "If you set goals and go after them with all the determination you can muster, your gifts will take you places that will amaze you." Setting goals correctly is so important to achieving your vision because it shifts the focus to your goals rather than your fears.

Everyone reading this will have a different starting point. No matter where yours is, your vision and goals can evoke a wide range of emotions. It is essential to follow the process to get the results we continue to discuss.

Think back to the dream home analogy we shared with you in Chapter 3; once you finish the home design, it can be built one brick at a time. Similarly, the pursuit of your vision is done one goal at a time, and it may take weeks, months, years, or even a lifetime to reach it. Even though some goals may take longer to accomplish, when you are pursuing your vision, you will likely feel and see an immediate shift in your internal motivation and outward productivity. Your vision provides direction and purpose, whereas the goals are the key milestones you strive for to make your vision a reality. The vision and goals come together harmoniously to create an inspired path forward.

We have observed that in many organizations, goals are talked about often but rarely used in a way that improves execution or that gets great results. More often than not, organizational goals are often missing key elements that would dramatically increase both performance and productivity. When goals are written and used correctly, they become something managers and employees can pursue with a strong focus and lead to significant improvements in performance and productivity.

Think back to our discussion about the archer in Chapter 2; it makes sense that to hit the bullseye, an archer first needs to identify their target. Once they have done so, they can aim and shoot. Individually and as part of a team, you too need to be able to identify your bullseye or target (Q2 areas of focus).

This is a good reminder for all of us that our focus determines our reality!

During the past nine years, we have researched the power and effectiveness of goals within the organizations we have worked with. We often do a pre- and post-assessment to measure results. One of the reasons for increased productivity in the organizations we have worked with is because of this goal-setting process. Roles and goals empower a person or team to identify the Q2 activities and then convert those Q2 areas of focus into well-written goals.

The other fascinating part of our organizational research is that we discovered that people are around 90 percent more likely to accomplish something if they have a well-written goal and plan. Imagine that: whether a person is focused on their health, a relationship, a revenue target, a sales goal, a production number, or any other important business target, they are 90 percent more likely to accomplish something if it is clearly written in the form of a goal! However, that statistic is *only* applied when the goal-setting process is followed and done correctly.

We have also discovered that less than 10 percent of employees have clearly written goals, and 83 percent of managers feel that their team members could do a better job developing and executing their goals.

This performance and execution gap is an excellent place for leaders to focus their attention. They can mentor their team members and give them the training to develop the big three skillset, which will almost always lead to a higher-performing team. We have seen firsthand that this is a skillset people can learn through practice and repetition. Like the Division I football coach we talked about earlier in the book, a manager cannot be frustrated with their team members if they haven't helped them develop the skillset in the first place.

A manager also needs to understand why a negative stigma is sometimes attached to goals and why people might be hesitant to develop their goals. One of the questions we asked people in our research is *Why haven't you set goals in the past?* We got a wide range of responses, but many of the same answers showed up repeatedly. Below are a few of the common reasons why many people don't set goals or are hesitant to put in the effort:

- It is something they never learned how to do in their home, high school, or university.

- Immediate accountability comes with a written goal, and sometimes that can be a scary thing depending on what the goal is.

- Often, they have a fear of failure with written goals because once written, they become real.

- Many recognize goals are important, but they simply haven't made the time to do it because they procrastinate or are too busy.

The majority of these concerns are the result of a lack of an actual process—which isn't their fault. These are all easily addressed when someone follows the simple flow outlined in the next chapter.

This goal-setting process goes back to the do what matters most mindset and skillset. When you align your goals with your vision, you are scheduling your priorities rather than prioritizing your schedule. It also does not matter what your current starting point is; in the spirit of *good, better, best*, this skillset will help anyone improve their performance and productivity from where they are today!

John and Bella

We have a friend named John who is an accountant and has several children. He has been successful in many ways and has always had a seemingly great life. However, we were talking one day, and he commented that he felt like he was in a lull. He admitted he had done well financially and accomplished many of the things he set out to do. Yet, he felt as if he could accomplish more and do more than he currently was. We asked him about goals, and he responded, "I have never really set personal goals. I've thought about a lot of things I want, but I have never written personal goals." We talked about roles and goals for a few minutes, and John decided to give it a try. That year, he developed five specific goals—just one for each role.

One of his goals was to run a 5k in less than thirty minutes before July 30th. Another, for his role in the accounting firm, was related to achieving a financial performance target; this target was a big jump from where his performance had been the previous year. To his amazement, he accomplished all five of his goals by the end of the year. In his words, he said, "I would not have done a single one of these five things had it not been for my written goals and pre-week planning." This experience made him a believer in the power and focus of roles and goals. The next year, he added more goals to each role, and he has continued to see significant growth in each area of his life. It took him 40 years, but he finally sat down and identified his Q2 areas of focus that mattered most to him. For our accountant friend, goals took the impossible and made it possible. He designated five targets, and he landed the arrow right in the bullseye for each one.

One of the frequent comments we receive from people is how roles and goals have helped in *every* area of their lives. In addition to personal and professional benefits, people often share stories of what happened when they shared this process with their children, their spouse, or other friends. To illustrate the point of how far-reaching roles and goals are, we will share an example of Rob's daughter Bella.

Each December, Rob's kids sit down and develop their roles and goals for the upcoming year. When they finish their goals, Rob and his wife reward each child with a fun gift or activity. One of Rob's daughters, Bella, was 11 years old when she came up with the role of author. Rob was surprised because she had never really talked about being an author. It was interesting to get a glimpse into her evolving mindset when she started to think outside the box.

After she finished her goals, Rob helped her make a few adjustments so that they were well-worded, and she was set up for success. In the role of author, she came up with the goal: *Write a children's book by December 20th*. Rob complimented Bella on setting a goal that would be fun and stretch her. A couple of months later, on a beautiful spring afternoon, they sat together on their lawn to review her goals. When they read that particular goal, she commented that she wasn't exactly sure how to go about it or where to start. So, they decided to write a book together as a fun father/daughter project.

They came up with an action plan of *who* would do *what* by *when*. Bella would do certain things, such as come up with the words, questions, and basic ideas for an illustration. Rob would find the illustrator and correspond back and forth to finalize the illustrations.

They came up with the title *A–Z: The Best in You and Me*. The idea was to go through each letter in the alphabet and choose a catchy word associated with that letter—for example, A = Attitude, B = Beautiful, C = Courage, and so on (you can see the other letters at BellasBook.net). They also decided that Bella would come up with a little quote associated with that word to put at the top of each page, and at the bottom of each page, they would add a question to stimulate a meaningful conversation between parent and child. Their vision was to create a book that would help parents or grandparents engage in conversation with their children or grandchildren. You can see an example in Figure 13 of "Beautiful." The question at the bottom of the page is *What are some beautiful things about you?*

During this process of creating the book, they encountered a few snags. For example, they had to go through 150 applications to choose the illustrator. The design of both Bella's book and the website dedicated to it had some hiccups, but Bella stuck with it—the goal kept her focused.

Eight months later, everything was complete. In mid-December, Rob and Bella were in a mad dash to finish the book in time to meet her goal. On December 20th, after a chaotic scramble to get the first copies printed, Rob and Bella stood on their back porch, holding the completed book in their hands (as shown in Figure 14).

Figure 13. A page from Bella's book

Figure 14. Bella's completed book

Since then, people from all over the world have read Bella's book. She made enough money from its sales to pay for soccer and dance and to start saving for college. More importantly, parents have shared stories with Bella about some great conversations they have had with their children while reading her book.

The reason we share this is that it all started with the roles and goals process. Bella came up with the role of author and the accompanying goal to *Write a children's book by December 20th.*

But what if she had not written that goal? *A–Z: The Best in You and Me* would not exist. Bella wouldn't have met some of the people she has met, she wouldn't have made that money, and she certainly would not have had some of the cool experiences she had along the journey.

The whole point is that if an 11-year-old can do it, anybody can do it!

Wrap Up

There is an old saying that goes, "Action without planning is wishful thinking."

You will feel a wide array of exciting emotions when you go through this process of identifying the goals that will help you shift your time and focus to Q2 and what matters most.

Imagine how great it would be to have your entire team focus on their roles and goals and what matters most in their job. Employees who go through this process tend to be the ones recognized for thinking outside the box and contributing to the team. They find new and better ways to do their jobs, serve the customer, and grow the organization. These are the types of results organizations should expect when their team members follow the process and do what matters most!

As the Cheshire Cat in Lewis Carroll's *Alice's Adventures in Wonderland* points out, "If you don't know where you are going, any road will get you there."[19]

When you arm yourself with your vision and goals, you will have the foundational plan so that you are extremely focused on what matters most. You know where you are going, and you have a plan to get there.

Now, let's get started on *your* roles and goals!

REFLECTION QUESTIONS FOR THIS CHAPTER:

1. Think about your own life. Why would it be beneficial for you to have roles and goals? Which of your roles do you feel would benefit from an increased focus?

2. What were your thoughts about goals while reading this chapter?

3. How could you help your coworkers or team members (or family) develop their roles and goals? What would the impact be?

6

How to Develop Roles and Goals

This approach to goal setting—roles and goals—helps a person maintain balance, increase performance and productivity, and identify what matters most.

In Chapter 4, you developed a vision for each role. The vision is the strategic focus or internal compass that gives you direction and purpose for each of your roles. The *roles and goals* are the operational focus and help you specifically identify your targets for this year. The goals are the specific milestones or areas of focus *this year* toward realizing your vision. Although the vision is a feeling and an emotion, the goals are specific, and measurable. It is this process of working toward goals and pre-week planning that ultimately connects your daily actions to your vision and what matters most. At the organizational level, we invite teams to develop both annual *and* quarterly goals. But, for this book, we will keep the focus solely on individual *annual* goals.

During your career, at some point, you were probably asked to develop professional goals for your position or department. Although that is a good start, roles and goals take it to another level. We invite you to take the intentions that you have likely thought about for years and turn them into specific goals—this will have a big impact on increasing your performance average.

In the following pages, we introduce the five steps to develop your annual goals effectively, and then we'll share some additional tips that will take a *good* goal and make it a *great* goal.

Five Steps to Develop Your Annual Goals

The following are the five steps to develop effective roles and goals. This process helps a person develop Q2 thinking and focus. When they follow these simple steps, it helps them identify their bullseye and what matters most. When a person has a clear target, well-written goals can dramatically increase performance and productivity. Once the person or team has a clear target (goal), they can develop a plan and get focused! Just by following these five steps, you will have done what less than 10 percent of people do.

1. Review your vision.

A person's goals should align with their vision. Rather than focus on the problem, we shift the playing field to the vision. The vision is the purpose or destination, and the goals are the path to make the vision a reality. If your goals align with your vision, they will be much more powerful and meaningful than if they were to stand alone.

2. Identify your roles.

Just as you did with your vision, in this step you identify the specific roles that matter most to you. For example, some of your roles might include manager, sales rep, parent, spouse/partner, friend, son/daughter, church member, or brother/sister. As a reminder, however, it is your personal role that is your most important role.

We break the personal role—and only the personal role—down into four separate subcategories, all related to your individual well-being: physical, mental, emotional, and spiritual. *Physical* involves taking care of your body, *mental* is developing your mind, *emotional* is taking care of your internal feelings of stress and well-being, and *spiritual* is often about your connection to divinity. Another way to look at these is to connect them to your body, mind, heart, and soul. It is essential to think about how you will take care of yourself in each of those four areas and put those thoughts into the form of a goal. For example, Gary's reading goal from Chapter 5 was in his personal (mental) role—to focus on developing his mind. The personal role is you taking care of yourself!

As we mentioned earlier, it is often easier to just think about our professional roles. However, it is thinking about your goals in the context of your different roles that helps you have a balance of success stories across each area of your life. When you divide your life into your most important roles, you can maintain balance and think about what you can do to achieve your vision in each role. This approach keeps a person focused on their priorities and what matters most (the Q2 area of the Do What Matters Most matrix).

3. Set SMART goals in each role.

At some point in your career, you have likely heard of the SMART acronym. Goals are *SMART* when they are specific, measurable, achievable, relevant, and time-specific.

The ability to write goals in a SMART way is one of the keys to effective goal setting and one of the most challenging areas to get right; it is a skillset. Like anything, the more practice a person gets with writing goals this way, the easier it becomes. The way you write your goal sets you up for either success or failure.

It was interesting to see a study conducted by Strava, a software company that tracks cycling and running exercises.[20] They tracked 98.3 million uploaded activities and observed that the most common date for people to ditch their New Year's resolution is January 19th—just under three weeks into the year. In the study, they also observed that although most quit on January 19th, 88 percent of runners who set a SMART goal were still running six months later.

The words you use and the way you write your goals matter! There is a big difference between *Get in better shape this year* and *Have a resting heart rate of 66 BPM by July 1st.*

On a team, each member should be able to identify the goals that matter most to them and write those in a SMART way. Establishing roles and goals is a skillset that every manager and employee would benefit from mastering because of the direct impact it will have on their performance and productivity.

Let's go a little deeper into the SMART acronym:

SPECIFIC

The more specific a goal is, the more likely a person is to achieve it. Which one of these examples do you think is better?

Lose weight, or *Be at 135 pounds by October 30th.*

Of course, the second example is better because it is specific and easier to develop a plan around. Furthermore, the second example is written in a positive way. Positive goals feel more achievable and are more motivating than negative ones. Notice how the example did not say *Lose 15 pounds*; instead it stated a specific target weight.

These little adjustments to the wording might seem obvious here. Still, it is common to see variations of the *lose weight* goal in the professional setting, and then people wonder why they do not see dramatic improvements. Wording matters!

MEASURABLE

At the end of the year, a person should be able to look back at their goals and objectively say, "Yes, I did" or "No, I didn't" accomplish them. Two words a person should never use when setting goals are *more* and *better*— or any variation of those vague words. A measurable goal increases accountability and is more likely to help you accomplish it.

Here are two examples to illustrate the difference between a measurable goal and one that is not:

Have a great relationship with my spouse versus *Average two dates a month without the children.*

or

Read more books versus *Read 12 nonfiction books by December 20th.*

The second example in both cases is a better goal because it is specific *and* measurable. The example of having a great relationship is a nice vision but a poor goal because it is neither specific nor measurable. Likewise, the first example in both cases allows for a lot of wiggle room, but the second examples keep a person accountable because they are either "yes" or "no" goals—they drive behavior and action.

ACHIEVABLE

Your goals should stretch you and potentially take you outside your comfort zone but still be achievable. It may not be realistic to set a goal of earning $10 million in the next six months if you're currently earning $1,000 a month. If a goal is unachievable or even just too difficult, a person is more likely to become discouraged and give up. Remember the rubber band discussion in Chapter 1? Our goals should stretch us, yet still be achievable. A phrase we like to use is that your goals should cause you to feel slightly uncomfortable. Slightly uncomfortable is a good balance between stretching and still being achievable.

The initial response from the sales team example in Chapter 1—when they were asked to go from 17 to 34 sales—was that they were slightly uncomfortable. That is the balance you are looking for, slightly uncomfortable, coupled with excitement and focus.

RELEVANT

Your goals should be relevant and aligned with your vision. If a part of your vision is *I am a healthy and well-rounded person*, then you would likely include specific goals about health and exercise. Your goals are the milestones toward achieving your vision.

TIME-SPECIFIC

If possible, add a date or time to your goal. For example, *Finish a 5k in less than 30 minutes by July 21st*, or *Average two dates a month*. When a time or date is attached to your goal, it increases accountability.

4. Send your goals to three to five people who you trust.

Once you develop your annual goals, send them to three to five people who you trust and admire. This is one of the keys to accountability. Several studies indicate that this step significantly increases the likelihood of a person accomplishing their goals. You can tell them why you are sending them your goals and then report back to them at the end of the year. We have shared our roles and goals for decades, and doing so has helped us form a tight bond with that circle of friends. Your peers will enjoy getting your goals as well as your report from the previous year, and you are often apt to find their feedback helpful.

We can tell you from firsthand experience that when we are waffling on whether to finish a goal halfway through the year, remembering this year-end reporting usually drives us to complete the goal.

Pause and think of a few people with whom you could share your goals. Whoever you are visualizing in your mind, do you look up to them, respect them, and admire them? If so, that is the type of accountability team you want.

This crucial step of sharing your goals will almost always increase the likelihood that you will accomplish them.

5. Reference your goals often.

Lastly, do not go through all the effort to develop your goals and then tuck them in a drawer. Put your goals in a place where you can see them often—maybe next to your bed or your computer—or write them in your weekly planner. In the next chapter, we will introduce the process of pre-week planning. The most successful people—those who see dramatic improvements in both productivity and performance—reference their goals weekly as part of their pre-week planning. The whole point is that we make our daily and weekly actions align with our goals and vision.

The Slight Edge of Goal Setting

There is a great book written by Jeff Olson titled *The Slight Edge*. The whole point of the book is that a couple of small tweaks or variations in almost anything can have a massive impact on the outcome; hence, the slight edge. Writing goals the right way is a similar concept. If you make a few small tweaks or variations to the old way of doing your goals, you can have a significant impact on the outcome. In the spirit of setting goals in a way that is powerful and drives a specific behavior, we invite you to throw away the term *New Year's resolution*. Instead of setting the proverbial New Year's resolution, which seems to fall apart so quickly, we want you to set yourself up for success in every goal that you write—this will keep you motivated and focused on what matters most. A few slight adjustments will change a vague New Year's resolution into a focused goal. The differences are slight and subtle, yet significant, and will give you an enormous edge over those who don't have this skillset!

Following the previous five steps will help a person develop clarity, focus, and balance. In addition to those five steps, we have found some other tips that give a person the slight edge to achieve their goals. Words matter, and the words you use in your goals will often mean the difference between success or failure—it is the seemingly small adjustments that are the slight edge. The subconscious mind is powerful, and if a person is "failing" on enough of their written goals, their subconscious mind will nudge them not to look at the goals because doing so brings out associated feelings of guilt. Instead, pick your words carefully. Then your subconscious mind can work for you when you use the five steps to goal setting and some of the following tips.

Here are a few guidelines that will set you up for success in your goal setting.

Rarely set daily goals.

When we visit with people and share this thought, a handful of people always skeptically raise their eyebrows . . . until we elaborate. In roles and goals, the focus is on your *annual* goals. The tactical focus comes during pre-week planning—in Chapters 7 and 8—and will help a person prioritize what matters most at the daily/weekly level, thereby eliminating the need for an annual goal that uses the word *daily*. For example, sometimes you hear people start the year and excitedly proclaim that their new goal is to *Exercise 30 minutes every day*. What they do not realize is that they likely just set themselves up for failure. If they miss a single day, they have already "failed" their goal as it was worded. With enough "failures," most people will then subconsciously avoid goals.

Instead, if such people make a couple of small adjustments to their goals, they can set themselves up for success. For example, they might word their goal this way: *Average four 30-minute workouts per week* or *Run a 10k by September 1st*. If we are talking about making sales instead of writing the goal, we might shift *Make 30 sales calls every day* to *Average 150 sales calls each week* or *Achieve $1.2M in sales by December 26th*. Notice the slight wording adjustments that provide a little flexibility in time and actions? The adjusted examples give a person added flexibility during the week while they still maintain the material integrity of what the goal is trying to accomplish.

This is not to say that a person cannot or should not break down a monthly or quarterly goal into daily targets. For example, if I want to make 20 sales per month, I would likely break that down into daily and weekly targets to achieve the monthly goal. We cover this in more detail in the next two chapters.

What we are saying is that because of pre-week planning, there are very few cases when a person should have a *daily* goal—a goal that fails if they miss a single day—as part of their annual goals.

Give yourself flexibility.

Think again about the previous example. A person who uses the daily sales goal of *Make 30 daily sales calls* only has to make fewer than 30 calls on one single day, for whatever reason, to fail at their goal. Instead, if they make a small adjustment in wording, they can maintain the same standard but have more flexibility. One way to do this is first to use the word *average*. At times the word average can be powerful in goal setting. If you go back to the previous tip's examples, you will see the word average used in a couple of different ways. In most cases, the goal *Average 30 sales calls per day* maintains the material integrity of the goal yet gives the person a little flexibility to be off on one or two days without "failing."

Another way to give yourself some more flexibility is to be careful with the words *every* and *at least*. There is a place for those words; you just need to be cautious using them. Instead of saying *every day* or *Do x at least x number of times*, you can stretch the time horizon on your goal. For example, Gary, from the last chapter, was going to initially write the goal *Read at least*

15 minutes every day. You can see no flexibility in Gary's original example and that it would only take him missing one day to fail at the goal.

Instead, with a small tweak, Gary changed the goal to *Average reading 1 leadership book per month*—which is what he did. He could have also written the goal as *Read 12 leadership books by December 26th*, and that would have also achieved the same objective. You might be thinking that it is still important to make time to read each day, and you are right. Gary used pre-week planning to allocate 15 minutes to read nearly every day, but as you would expect, he did miss a few days. When the goal was written as *Average reading 1 leadership book per month*, it still maintained the intent of the goal, and it set Gary up for success by giving him some flexibility. Remember, pre-week planning will connect each of your goals down to the daily and weekly level.

Set one to four goals in each role.

The intent is to focus on what matters most. If *everything* matters, then nothing matters. Keeping it to one to four goals per role will help you decide what matters most in each role. If this is the first time you are writing your goals, maybe you can just start with one goal per role. If you have been using goals for years, then maybe you can come up with three or four goals per role.

Remember that *performance* is hitting the bullseye. Your goal defines the bullseye, and at first, you want to focus on getting your arrow right on the mark—accomplishing your goal for that role. That is, hitting the bullseye, one arrow at a time. As you get good at doing so with one arrow, it will become more manageable, and you will find that you can add one to three more goals per role; then you'll find that your productivity goes up as well. Before you know it, you will be getting three to four arrows in each bullseye like a professional archer! Your performance and productivity will go up exponentially. But this progress starts with the focus you need to get the one arrow right on the mark. That is the first step.

In most cases, more than four goals per role detracts from the whole point of this process: to help a person focus their time and energy on what matters most. For best results, get laser-focused on the one goal that really matters most to you in each role.

At the end of the process, you should feel a combination of excitement, focus, and being slightly uncomfortable.

If you didn't take the free personal performance and productivity assessment that we discussed in the introduction, you can do it now; it only takes a few minutes, and it will give you a great snapshot of where you are today in your personal role (physically, mentally, emotionally, and spiritually). You can access the assessment at BYBassessment.com. This assessment assists you in pinpointing areas of focus so that you can identify the most meaningful goals for each role.

Aim for 70 to 80 percent accomplishment.

This seems to be the right balance of stretching one's self. If a person easily accomplishes all of their goals, they likely could have stretched themselves further. If a person only accomplished 20 to 30 percent of their goals, they likely had more than one to four goals, did not word them correctly, or did not do pre-week planning. A 70 to 80 percent accomplishment rate at year-end usually correlates to a dramatic jump in performance and productivity, as well as a sense of accomplishment. If you did not hit 100 percent, that is often a good thing, and you should be able to pat yourself on the back. Remember, in the spirit of good, better, best, your roles and goals for the following year will give you a chance to renew your focus and decide on new goals for each role.

Plan for one to three hours to finish your roles and goals.

It will usually take a person between one and three hours to finish their roles and goals. We invite you to block time in your calendar right now to go through this process. Procrastination is one of the most insidious success killers, and many people, through the years, have never made it past the phase of good intentions. Hence, the best time to start is right now, while it is fresh on your mind.

Og Mandino, author of *The Greatest Salesman in the World*, wisely said "I will not avoid the tasks of today, for I know that tomorrow never comes.

Let me act now even though my actions may not bring happiness or success, for it is better to act and fail than not to act and flounder."[21]

In business, *return on investment (ROI)* is one of the most important indicators to track. Developing your roles and goals is an investment into yourself and will yield a tremendous ROI. One to three hours is a small price to pay for an improved, successful life. Wouldn't you agree?

Do this with your partner or team.

If your partner or team is willing to participate, you can begin to imagine how much more powerful it will be when everyone is aligned using a similar process. When you have a team made up of members who have each developed their roles and goals, and who each consistently do pre-week planning, it creates unity, alignment, and accountability.

Visit BYBgoals.com for a free roles and goals template.

When you sign up at our website, we will send you two templates. One is a blank template for your roles and goals; the other is a template filled in with examples of well-worded goals (see Figure 15). You can reference this template to look at various SMART goal examples (the template with examples is identical to what you see in Figure 15).

Practice

Imagine that a person wants to learn how to play basketball, but they have never touched an actual basketball. If you spend all day talking about basketball with that person, but they still do not touch a basketball, they likely will not improve. Wouldn't you agree that a person needs to practice dribbling, shooting, and so on if they want to get better? Like anything, if we want to develop a new skillset, it takes practice.

In the spirit of practice and repetition, let's go through a few examples focused on creating SMART goals and using some of the other slight edge tips.

Figure 15. Example template for vision and goals

VISION AND GOALS FOR 202X

	PERSONAL (Physical, Mental, Emotional, Spiritual)
Role:	
Vision:	I choose to live a balanced, healthy lifestyle and I am in great physical shape. I maintain a high level of spirituality and my relationship with God is of the utmost importance. I am financially free with no debt or financial obligations to anyone. I am disciplined, focused, and put in the effort to do what matters most!
Annual Goals:	Physical: Run a 10k by September 1st. Average 72 BPM by July 1st.
	Mental: Read at least 12 improvement/motivation books before Dec 30th.
	Emotional: Average two yoga sessions per week.
	Spiritual: Read the Old Testament before Dec 30th.

	MANAGER
Role:	
Vision:	I am a transformational leader who knows the stories of my team members. I invest in whatever resources I can to give my team the best training and help them reach their fullest potential. I'm the type of leader they would support and follow without the title!
Annual Goals:	1 Finalize the strategic plan for our division by February 1st.
	2 Do a Continue-Start-Stop with all employees by April 1st.
	3 Achieve $1.5M in sales by December 27th.
	4 Acquire 15 new customer contracts by June 1st.

	PARENT
Role:	
Vision:	I am an example in thought and deed of what a true gentleman looks like. I am the type of person I want my daughters to marry. I am present with my children and we constantly develop great memories together. I help them see their potential and how they can make a difference in the world. I am vulnerable and I empathize with them.
Annual Goals:	1 Average one family weekend trip within five hours of our home every other month.
	2 Take each kid on at least one, one-on-one trip before Dec 30th.
	3 Help each child finish their Roles and Goals by January 10th.
	4 Average one fun daddy/daughter (son) date night per month.

	SPOUSE OR PARTNER
Role:	
Vision:	I am a kind and caring husband who always helps Tonya feel like a 10. I am totally faithful in thought and action and I constantly strive to compliment her, serve her, and be the husband of her dreams!
Annual Goals:	1 Read Start with the Vision together and go through the Six-Step Process for our relationship by July 1st.
	2 At least two weekend getaway trips together before December 30th.
	3 Average two dates a month without the children.
	4 Finalize a family vision by March 1st.

Imagine that you are a manager or coworker and you are mentoring one of your team members to improve their goals. How would you rephrase each of these examples to make them a well-written goal?

- *Be a better neighbor.*

- *Exercise every day to get in better shape.*

- *Be a better manager.*

- *Be healthier this year and lose more weight.*

- *Improve sales and do a better job closing deals.*

- *Get better feedback from my team.*

- *Spend more quality time with my partner.*

Now, think about how you would reword each goal to make it SMART and set the person up for success. For example, notice how the words *more* and *better* kept showing up; those two words should never be seen in goals because they are neither specific nor measurable. What would you change to improve the wording of these goals?

The following list shows variations for each of the goals from the previous list. Notice how these are both specific and measurable:

- *Have at least one neighborhood gathering at our house before September 1st.*

- *Average three strength workouts per week.*

- *Finish the annual strategic plan for the marketing division by January 7th.*

- *Run a 5k in less than 28 minutes before July 30th* or *Average a resting heart rate of less than 73 bpm by August 1st.*

- *Average 46 sales calls per week* or *Achieve $642,000 in sales by December 26th.*

- *Do an anonymous continue–start–stop with our team before March 1st.*

- *Average two dates a month without the children.*

Remember, words matter! How you write the goal becomes critical to the focus you want to have and whether it gets done.

Wrap Up

If you are reading this in November or December, you can start developing your goals for the coming year. If you are reading this in any other month, we encourage you to develop your roles and goals for the remainder of this year.

Look at your roles and goals through the lens of the ping pong balls and the aquarium from Chapter 2. When the teacher put the ping pong balls in the aquarium before the pebbles, sand, or water, there was plenty of room. When the teacher put the water in the aquarium first, there was no room for the ping pong balls. Like the teacher in this experiment, you want to prevent the small things from crowding out the big things. The idea is to proactively identify the things that matter most and put them in the form of a goal so that they do not get crowded out by the daily fires or the next shiny object.

Let's finish this chapter with some variations of the questions we used in the beginning:

- What would you like to accomplish this year?

- What are your targets for this year, both personally and professionally?

- How will you specifically measure success in your different roles?

- What are some ways you could significantly increase performance and productivity within your workplace? How can you measure those things?

- When will you finish your roles and goals?

- Where will you put your roles and goals so that you see them often? Suggestion: Use the front of your Becoming Your Best weekly planner.

- Who will you share your goals with, and when will you share them?

These are the questions to get you started. We invite you to get the roles and goals template, block off time on your calendar to work on fleshing it out, and commit to a time when you will finish it and share your roles and goals with others. Once you finish, print your roles and goals, and put them in a place where you will see them often.

Now, it is time to move to pre-week planning—what we consider to be the most important habit because it brings everything together and turns your vision and goals into a reality at the daily and weekly level!

REFLECTION QUESTIONS FOR THIS CHAPTER:

1. What was the experience of developing your roles and goals like for you?

2. What are your most important roles?

3. What are one to four goals you have for each of those roles?

4. Who else do you know who would benefit from going through this process to develop their roles and goals (son/daughter, partner, team member)? Why would this process be helpful to them?

5. If you choose to share your roles and goals, who will you share them with?

7

The Power of Pre-week Planning

Before a pilot jumps into the cockpit, they will always do their *pre-flight planning*. In the fighter pilot world, it takes between one and ten hours to plan a single mission, depending on its complexity. Pre-flight planning includes researching the target or destination; planning the route of flight; checking the weather, the aircraft maintenance records; and so on.

Imagine what would happen if a pilot said, "Forget it, we don't need to do our pre-flight planning; we're just going to wing it today!" In the fighter pilot world, that would result in chaos, misalignment, and confusion—not good!

How many times do people go into their week without a plan and expect a different result? Just as *pre-flight planning* is critical for a pilot, *pre-week planning* is just as essential when people want to take control of their lives and do what matters most. If a pilot wants to be successful, they do their pre-flight planning. How much more successful would a person be if they approached their professional and personal lives like a pilot—doing their pre-week planning every week before they start the week? When it comes to performance and productivity, pre-week planning is the *keystone* (the most important stone in an arch); pre-week planning is what drives the vision and goals to become a reality. Pre-week planning is the key to scheduling your priorities rather than prioritizing your schedule.

If you met us on the street one day and asked, "What's one habit that would change my life—guaranteed?" our answer, 100 percent of the time, would be pre-week planning. When people develop this habit, they share that, indeed, it changed their lives for the better. Productivity and performance increase; health and relationships improve; stress and task saturation decrease.

In the spirit of *good, better, best,* we invite you to see how pre-week planning can enhance and improve whatever planning approach you are using today. If a person has been using sticky notes or a running to-do list, pre-week planning will take it to the next level. No matter what your position or title, everyone in an organization will benefit from the simplicity of pre-week planning.

Years ago, we met with the executive team from one of the largest PepsiCo distributors in the United States. Each executive developed a draft of their written personal vision, as well as their roles and goals. The energy and excitement in the room were palpable!

We moved into pre-week planning and went through each step. Each person then took between five and ten minutes to do their pre-week planning for the week. One of the executives, who we will call John, wrote in the role of parent, "Call my son." This executive was in his late 50s to early 60s. He was a seasoned executive and had been with PepsiCo for decades.

It was not abnormal to see someone write "Call my son" in that type of role; nonetheless, we asked him why he specifically wrote that. He responded, "Because I haven't talked with my son in over seven years!" It was apparent this was an issue that had weighed on him for a long time. He continued, "My son and I got into an argument seven years ago, and we haven't spoken since." Wow!

We asked him when he would make the call that week, and he responded, "I'll call him Wednesday evening." We then invited him to physically write it in his weekly planner for Wednesday at 7:00 p.m., which he did.

Six months later, we had a follow-up workshop with this same executive team. We were so excited to catch up with John to see if he made the call. When we walked into the room, he jumped out of his chair to come over and greet us. We shook his hand and asked him, "So, did you make the call?" He responded enthusiastically, "I was scared to death to pick up the phone that evening. I had no idea whether or not my son would even talk with me." He continued, "But, I made the call. It was amazing because as soon as we started talking, we realized neither of us could remember what we had argued about seven years ago. Now, we talk every week, and we're best friends!" He went on to share that he discovered, in that initial call, that he had two grandchildren who he did not even know existed. Although it is sad that it took that long, at least John made the call!

It was interesting to hear some of John's additional thoughts. He commented, "For years, I knew I needed to make that call, but like many things, I woke up every morning thinking I would just do it the next day. Weeks turned into months, and months turned into years. I intended to make the call, but I always seemed to be too busy, so I just kept putting it off until later." He also said, "Since I've repaired that relationship, it's like my entire world has changed. I am much more focused as an executive. I am a better leader, and I have a renewed energy that was not there before! It's as if an invisible weight lifted from my shoulders." He concluded by saying, "Without pre-week planning, I probably would have never made that call. Pre-week planning changed my life in almost every way!"

There are a lot of Johns in the world—they all have different scenarios but the same challenge. People are looking for ways to move into Q2 (being proactive) and do what matters most in many parts of their lives.

Remember, in our research of more than 1,260 managers and executives, 68 percent felt that prioritizing their time was their number one challenge. Yet, 80 percent did not have a process to do so. Vision, goals, and *especially* pre-week planning are the answer to close that statistical productivity gap!

Performance and Productivity

Earlier in the book, we said that a person who finishes their vision and goals and is disciplined about pre-week planning would see an average increase in performance and productivity of 30 to 50 percent. That is only partly true. The real improvement is actually much higher than that!

Figure 16 shows the results of our study of managers and executives who did pre-week planning for five weeks. It is important to note that these results came *after* the participants developed their vision and goals. In other words, pre-week planning was done in alignment with the vision and goals rather than as an isolated event. It is also important to note that most managers and executives who participated in this study had been doing some form of planning before doing pre-week planning. However, they did not feel like what they were doing was very effective—it usually included sticky notes, to-do lists, or other forms of Q1 reactive planning (and it usually *only* focused on their work schedule).

The vertical axis in Figure 16 tracks weekly goals or activities, and the horizontal axis references the number of weeks tracked. The rising line on the top represents weekly goals or activities *scheduled* as part of pre-week planning, and the rising line on the bottom represents the weekly goals or activities *accomplished* at the end of the week.

After you look at Figure 16, we will share some interesting findings that reveal what happens with the majority of people who start pre-week planning.

Figure 16. The results of pre-week planning for one month

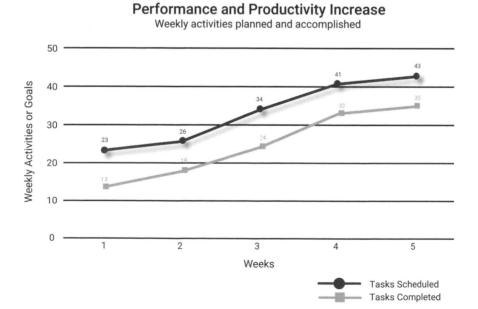

Here are some key takeaways from our research:

1. Like anything, pre-week planning is a skillset. The more we do it, the better we become at it. With each repetition, it becomes easier and takes less effort.

   If a person is learning a new technique, such as how to catch a football, that technique will not be perfect on the very first catch. It takes numerous repetitions of doing it the *right* way before the new technique is done well and becomes a part of the person's habits.

   Take a look at Figure 16. You see an average of 23 weekly goals or activities scheduled for the first week; this number swells to 41 by the fourth week. Again, as in the football example, this is the result of practice. When people do pre-week planning for one or two weeks, their brains naturally get used to it and the ideas flow a lot easier. With time, they think of more ideas and become more creative in each role, hence the increase in performance and productivity. This familiarity with pre-week planning is why teams see a significant increase in engagement, performance, and productivity during the first 30 days after implementing these new habits.

   Because developing a new habit is a function of consistency and repetition, we encourage people to commit to pre-week planning for an entire year. Once pre-week planning becomes a habit, you will never want to live without it!

2. The number of weekly goals and activities *accomplished* will dramatically increase in the first month of pre week planning. Like we said with the first point, the first couple of weeks are for developing a new process and habit. In this timeframe, people are figuratively tiptoeing into the water to see what works and what does not. After the first week or two, the experimentation phase is over, they get used to the process, and they identify what works for them.

Take another look at Figure 16. Notice that in the first week, only an average of 13 weekly goals or activities were accomplished, and by the fourth week, that number more than doubled to 33. This shows that when pre-week planning is done for just one month consistently and correctly, it can cause over a 100 percent average increase in performance and productivity.

Additionally, if you track it weekly, pre-week planning averages a productivity increase of 15 to 30 percent week over week in the first four weeks. This type of focus on doing what matters most is why so many people and teams love pre-week planning!

3. Overall, performance and productivity were significantly higher when combined with roles rather than just a professional focus. The overall increase in productivity makes sense when you think about it. When a person makes time to exercise, read, meditate, and so on, it seems evident that other areas of that person's life will also improve. You have probably experienced this yourself when you have taken care of *you*. It is a lot easier to show up for your team, coworkers, and clients when your own house is in order. The term we used earlier in the book for this was *performance average*. When a person does pre-week planning by roles, it will increase their performance average—almost every area of their life will improve.

The focus on overall well-being may seem obvious, but for many people, things like exercise, reading, and meditation seem to slip through the cracks. But when a person shifts to Q2 thinking and planning, they make time for what matters most, and overall productivity goes up as a result.

4. In just one month, the gap between weekly goals and activities *planned* and *accomplished* narrows significantly. In Figure 16, in the first week of pre-week planning, only 56 percent of the planned weekly goals and activities were completed; however, by the fourth week, 80 percent were accomplished.

We have found that accomplishing between 70 and 80 percent of weekly goals and activities is optimal. Q1 fires will always pop into the week and require you to shift your schedule. But that flexibility and shifting is an expected part of the week, and you have planned for it as part of your pre-week planning. The expectation we set is to rarely plan to accomplish 100 percent of your planned weekly goals and activities. If you are the type of person who likes to check every square and cross off every item, give yourself permission to be flexible and adjust during the week.

Pre-week planning will help people shift from Q1—a reactive approach—to the proactive approach in Q2 of focusing on what matters most. The Q2 shift translates into an increased feeling of satisfaction and accomplishment as well as reduced stress.

5. Finally, as mentioned before, pre-week planning is much more effective when you align it with your vision and goals rather than as an isolated event. When you finish your vision, develop your goals, and then reference them weekly as part of pre-week planning, you are doing what less than 1 percent of people do consistently. That is why we are so confident in our promise that the big three will be life-changing regardless of a person's starting point.

Although it is always nice to see the research and statistical side of these three powerful habits, the real benefit comes when you see the transformation happening to those on your team and in your family, and especially when you see it happening in your personal life. Every one of those "numbers" you see in the weekly goals or action items represents a meaningful activity or task you have accomplished. Every number represents something you've done to better the team, further the growth of the organization, improve your health, improve a relationship, or any other host of essential activities.

Allow us to share our friend Rich's story. He worked for Schluter Systems, a leader in installation systems for tile and stone. Shortly after he started on the big three, he sent us a handwritten note. We have summarized his comments here to illustrate what happens when a person applies the habits of vision, roles and goals, and pre-week planning together:

> My name is Rich, and I met you about a year ago at our Schluter meeting in Florida. You trained over 100 of us. One of the first things you said at our event was that this day was going to "change my life!" At 64, this old dog can be rather skeptical. I am also one of Schluter's workshop presenters and felt that making such a claim to a large group is tough to pull off. But our leaders were willing to invest in me, so I decided to get their money's worth!
>
> You talked about the five most important things to a long and healthy life, and I was only doing three of those things. The two I wasn't focused on were meditation and sleep. As a result of vision, goals, and pre-week planning, I enrolled in a meditation training course and have been practicing it twice a day.
>
> Also, getting eight hours of sleep has always been impossible for me, and it seems harder the older I get. I set a goal to get a sleep test and investigate my options. It was determined that I have sleep apnea, so I recently got a CPAP device. Yes, it HAS been a game-changer! I'm sleeping better than ever and have a lot more energy throughout the day.
>
> The vision, goals, and pre-week planning helped me focus on what matters most and make important changes in my life! Thank you.

Rich had these ideas and intentions floating around in his mind for years, but it was the combination of the big three (and his willing mindset) that moved him to take action.

Another woman we know named Nicole is a commercial designer with several young children at home. We shared the big three with Nicole and her husband Jay. Both commented that their marriage had suffered because of all the demands of life. Her personal life was also affecting her professional life. She was not responding to people's business inquiries as she should, and her business was suffering as a result. She was losing clients, she felt task saturated, and she was constantly in Q1; she was in a challenging phase of life.

After learning about the big three, Nicole and Jay decided to implement them. Both have finished their visions and roles and goals and have consistently done pre-week planning (with only a few misses). Nicole shared that when she does pre-week planning, she is on top of her game, her productivity is high, and she experiences minimal stress. Client relationships and referrals have improved, and she has seen major growth in her business. During the handful of weeks when Nicole did not do pre-week planning, she was stressed, anxious, and unproductive. This process has literally been a life-changer for Nicole and Jay. They credit the big three with transforming their marriage and bringing the flame back into their relationship. They were living in Q1, and when they learned about the big three, they shifted to Q2 and purposefully focused on what matters most.

Another example of the powerful impact of pre-week planning is from Michelle, a certified trainer and an executive in a global organization based in the UK. She said the following:

> It's hard to believe that I started doing this only a year ago. A major change in my life is pre-week planning. I have always done planning and have always had a "to-do" list, but it was never tied to my vision and goals (especially by role). I created a personal vision and goals that supported each of my roles. I have been doing that for a year and I just finished using my first weekly planner. I can honestly say that I am more focused now and accomplishing things that were always important, but that I put off or never got around to doing. I have focused time each week on the things that are important to me and are moving me toward the accomplishment of my goals and supporting my personal vision.
>
> Things just seem to start coming into being since I created my vision and have been doing the pre-week planning. I just smile to myself now every time something happens to move me toward my goals without a clear explanation.
>
> I've ordered books and planners for my team and family. I even gave one to my son, who is in his early 20s, and see him now doing pre-week planning with a very well-defined vision and goals for himself. Amazing things are happening for him as well because of this focus. If you are a parent of a college grad, you know how exciting this is!

We could fill a book with emails from people who have shared the impact the big three have had in their lives. The hope in sharing these experiences is to foster a belief and confidence that you can do it. Anyone who has the right mindset (a desire and discipline) can learn this skillset, and it will be transformational.

Before we jump into how to do pre-week planning, it is essential to remember that it is all three of these habits together that create a chemistry of excellence. Pre-week planning is undoubtedly a game-changer, yet it is exponentially more powerful when aligned with the vision and goals. The hope is that by this point, you have already put some serious thought into your vision and goals. When you finish them, it is pre-week planning that aligns your daily and weekly activities with accomplishing your goals. Pre-week planning is the galvanizer of the three habits. It is the process that takes the vision and goals to the daily and weekly level where tangible progress is made.

Pre-week Planning Basics

First, it is important to understand that pre-week planning is a process. Because it is a process, you can make adjustments and additions that work for you. The core process of pre-week planning is what makes it so powerful. However, if you feel you want to add certain things—such as writing a daily gratitude or lessons learned—you can certainly customize this process to what works best for you. We have invested thousands of hours of research to narrow the core process down to a few simple steps.

Before jumping into those steps, it is also important to note that some people like to use a paper planner while others use an online calendar. It does not matter what you use; it is the *process* that is important. The pre-week planning process stays the same, regardless of whether you use the online or paper approach.

For those of you who like a physical planner, our weekly planner supports the habit of pre-week planning. This planner has a place for your personal vision and roles and goals, and it provides a weekly view for pre-week planning for all 52 weeks. You can choose a planner with dates, or you can go with the undated option, whichever works best for you. A physical planner is simply a tool that helps a person develop the habit more easily and reinforces the accountability of the process.

So, whether you use our physical planner or an online calendar, it is common to wonder when the best time to do pre-week planning is. We suggest that you choose a time that works best for you and then be consistent with that time. The process typically takes between 20 and 45 minutes, and most people set aside a block of time between Friday afternoon and Sunday evening (assuming a standard work schedule) to do it. If they wait until Monday morning, most people find that it is too late—the firestorm of the week has already started, and Q1 is staring them in the face. Having said that, if for some reason you do not do your pre-week planning during the weekend, it is better to do it on Tuesday or Wednesday for the remainder of the week than not do it at all.

We invite you—right now—to think about the time that works best for you and set an alarm or reminder on your phone. In that reminder, type the words "pre-week planning." The alarm will serve as a reminder to connect the intention with the development of the new habit. The people who set the alarm or reminder are much more likely to be consistent and develop the habit of pre-week planning.

Lastly, people often wonder about pre-week planning with their coworkers and teams. For those doing pre-week planning as a team, we have found that it is much more effective if the entire team has finished their pre-week planning before Monday morning. We invite almost every team we work with to have a weekly alignment meeting to start the week and ensure everyone is going in the same direction. The teams that hold such a meeting and have everyone do their pre-week planning *before* that meeting are very aligned and in sync with each other. These teams tend to spend between 60 and 75 percent of their time in Q2 and a much smaller percentage in Q1 and Q3. The result? Significantly higher performance, productivity, and alignment with the team.

Pre-week Planning Is a Game-Changer!

Earlier, we indicated that during the first month, a person is likely to see at least a 30 to 50 percent increase in performance and productivity. Think about what that means for you as well as the other members of your team. From the professional side, this translates into better leadership, a higher-producing person or team, higher profitability, a better workplace environment, a more aligned team, increased sales, an improved culture, and a more engaged workforce. On the personal side, it translates into improved health, better relationships, alignment with your true authentic self, increased balance, and a deeper sense of peace and focus.

People we have worked with appreciate the stories of ordinary people who started doing pre-week planning and the impact it had on their lives. These stories suddenly make everything relatable, they spark new ideas, and they give people the confidence and enthusiasm to commit to pre-week planning. In that same spirit, we would like to share just a few stories with you about how pre-week planning has helped ordinary people do seemingly small things that have led to extraordinary results.

Our first story is about a woman named Christine. She told us that she meant to take her daughter on a special date to celebrate her birthday, which was in September. She was telling us this story in March, and she still had not taken her daughter on that special date—six months after her daughter's birthday! Christine commented that time had simply slipped away from her and that she had been "too busy."

She obviously didn't feel good about missing the birthday date, so she was thrilled to learn about pre-week planning. Christine was searching for something that could help her prioritize her time and get out of the daily Q1 routine. She was confident that this would be the answer that would help her take control of her schedule so that this kind of missed opportunity would not happen again.

After just three weeks of doing pre-week planning, she sent a message saying, "I love this! It is the first time I don't feel stressed, and I'm accomplishing more than I ever thought possible. It is relatively easy, and it has made a huge difference. You will be happy to know that I took my daughter on the long-overdue mommy/daughter date, and it was awesome. *Thank you, thank you!"*

How many times have you felt like Christine? There was something important you were supposed to do, but it slipped away and you never did it. Pre-week planning not only had an impact on Christine, but it also affected her daughter. How important do you think that date was to the daughter?

In another case, we were in Kigali, Rwanda, doing a workshop for several hundred Rwandans—some were college students, and others were successful business leaders. It was an incredible experience for us to be there with such an extraordinary group of people. Twenty-five years prior to this workshop, this country experienced a terrible genocide in which more than one million Rwandans were killed.

During our visit, we had the chance to meet privately with the president of Rwanda and hear about the incredible transformation the country has experienced since the genocide. It has transformed into a country of opportunity. At the time of this writing, it is the fifth safest country in the world, it is the second-fastest growing economy in all of Africa, and there has been an unprecedented alignment within the country. Needless to say, it is an extraordinary place, and it was a privilege to be there.

The attendees at our conference were from a wide range of experience and backgrounds. Among those who attended was a young manager in his twenties named Samuel Yesashimwe. He stood out to us as someone who was serious and would do whatever it took to succeed. Several months after we met in Rwanda, he wrote us an email and said the following:

> Learning about the big three was a life-changing experience. I am usually an organized person, but since I learned about the big three, I have taken it to the next level. I have finished my vision, goals, and consistently done pre-week planning. It has increased my productivity by at least 30 percent, and the results are incredible. In April, I was given a promotion and led the IBM CSC Program in Rwanda. Because it was new and there was so much to do, I probably would have failed without the excellent planning and management skills.
>
> On a personal level, one of the exercises during the conference was to develop our roles and goals for the year. I had always wanted to attend

graduate school in another country but didn't think it could happen to me. I had three schools in mind: Stanford, Oklahoma Christian University, and London Graduate School of Business.

I would like to tell you that *today is my first day in the MBA program at Oklahoma Christian University.*

There is so much that happened when I applied these tools. May God bless you!

When we received this email from Samuel, we were elated for him.

Samuel knew what he wanted, and it had been in the back of his mind for a long time. We have all procrastinated and put off things we knew were important; likewise, Samuel kept pushing these important ideas back month after month and year after year. It is when he focused on the big three that he finally took action. He developed a goal to send in applications to all three schools by October 1st. Every week, as part of pre-week planning, he did something toward accomplishing that goal. For example, one week he collected letters of recommendation, the next he wrote the required essay letters, and the next he had someone review his applications. It was the combination of vision, goals, and pre-week planning that helped Samuel focus on what mattered most and finally take action to go after it. His vision was clear, he had specific goals to achieve to realize his vision, and pre-week planning helped him stay ahead of the curve—in Q2—to achieve the goals.

We will share one final example that is personal to us. Steve has been doing pre-week planning for almost 40 years, and Rob has been doing it for about 24 years. Just as it has been life-changing for thousands of others, it has been life-changing for us as well. In fact, we would go as far as to say that without our vision, goals, and pre-week planning, our lives would be total chaos.

About a year ago, Rob flew to Indianapolis to do a keynote for 300 entrepreneurs and business leaders. During his pre-week planning that week, Rob wrote in the role of father, *Write a note to Lana.* Every week he comes up with something to do for or with his kids, and for Lana this week, it was to write her a note.

It was a beautiful blue-sky morning, and Lana had just walked out the door to go to school. Rob quickly took a minute to write her a note telling her how much he loved her and left it on her bed, then he got in his car and left for the airport.

The next evening, Rob was getting on the plane to fly home. It was already late in the evening, and he would not get home until around midnight. Rob had just sat down in his seat when his phone buzzed, and he saw an incoming text from his wife. He pulled out his phone and read the text. "I know you'll get home late, and the house will be dark, so I don't want you to miss this special note from Lana. She snuck into our room and left it on our headboard." (See Figure 17.)

Figure 17. Lana's note

It was a special moment for Rob, and he felt a tear slide gently down his cheek. He thanked his wife for the text and put away his phone. No matter what great things had happened that day, none of them topped this note from his daughter.

This back-and-forth note exchange continued for several weeks and became a fun game for them.

The reason we share this is that it took Rob less than one minute to write that note to Lana. It was the short, meaningful note exchange that created some great memories. Would Rob have written this note without pre-week planning? Probably not!

How many opportunities do we have to do seemingly simple things like that? What is the long-term impact of those seemingly small things?

We are far from perfect, which is all the more reason why we benefit so much from vision, goals, and pre-week planning. It is these three habits that will help anyone focus on what matters most and proactively schedule their priorities.

Wrap Up

Zig Ziglar wisely said, "I believe that being successful means having a balance of success stories across the many areas of your life. You can't truly be considered successful in your business life if your home life is in shambles." We believe the spirit of what Zig is saying is that a person's performance average will increase when they have a balance of success stories. Remember John (the PepsiCo executive)? When he resolved that relationship issue with his son, every area of his life improved.

Leaders and employees are craving a process to help them organize their time and do what matters most. Pre-week planning—in conjunction with establishing a vision and goals—is the process of closing that gap and dramatically improving the performance and productivity of a team.

The combination of the big three is what will empower a person to take ownership of their life and lead a life by design.

In the next chapter, we will go through the process of *how* to do pre-week planning!

REFLECTION QUESTIONS FOR THIS CHAPTER:

1. How could pre-week planning impact your life?

2. What were your thoughts on time and pre-week planning while reading this chapter?

3. What would be the impact of helping your coworkers or team members prioritize their time with pre-week planning?

8

How to Do Pre-week Planning

There are four simple steps to pre-week planning. You can reference the blank weekly planner template in Figure 18 or a completed template in Figure 19 while we go through each of these steps.

For those who would like a free pre-week planning template so that you can practice while reading this chapter, go to BYBGoals.com and print the pre-week planning template. You can follow along with each step and see how effective this process is in your own life.

Figure 18. Blank pre-week planning template

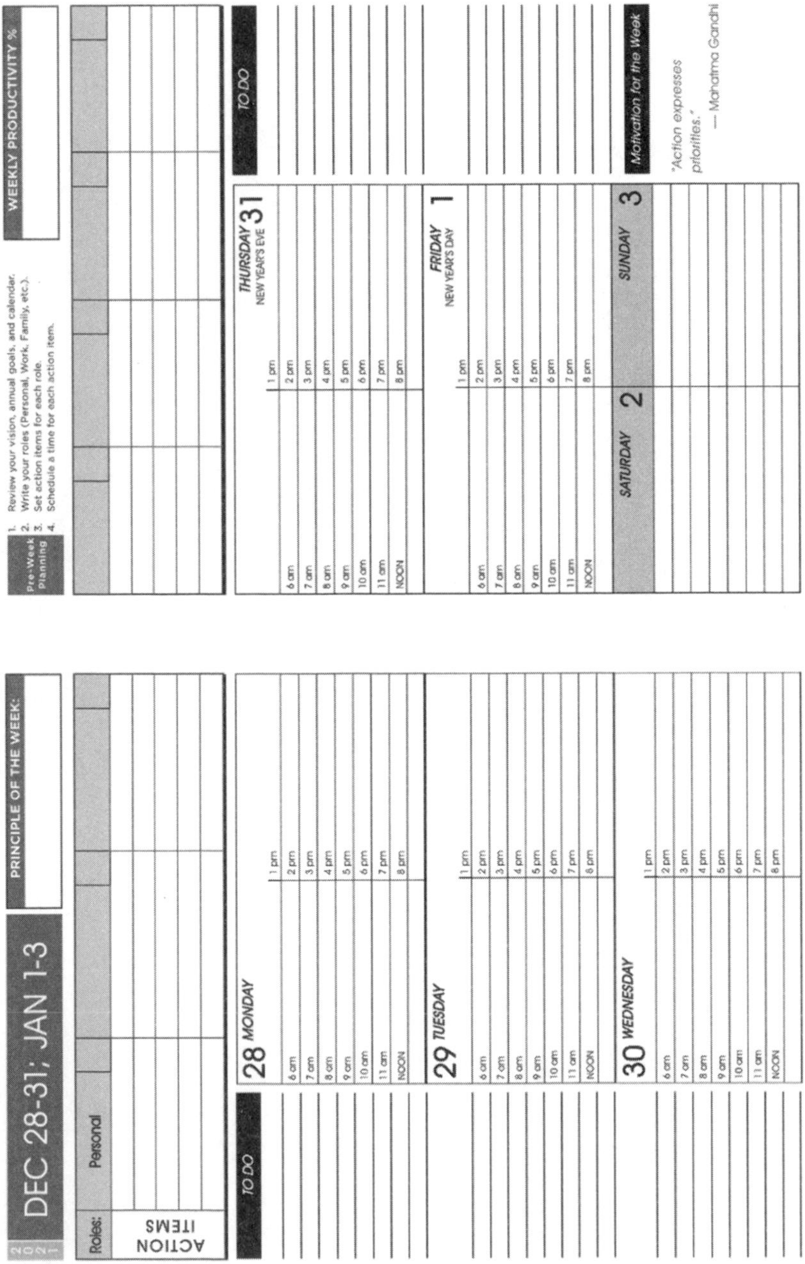

WEEKLY PRODUCTIVITY %

Pre-Week Planning
1. Review your vision, annual goals, and calendar.
2. Write your roles (Personal, Work, Family, etc.).
3. Set action items for each role.
4. Schedule a time for each action item.

TO DO

THURSDAY 31
NEW YEAR'S EVE

1 pm
2 pm
3 pm
4 pm
5 pm
6 pm
7 pm
8 pm

6 am
7 am
8 am
9 am
10 am
11 am
NOON

FRIDAY 1
NEW YEAR'S DAY

1 pm
2 pm
3 pm
4 pm
5 pm
6 pm
7 pm
8 pm

6 am
7 am
8 am
9 am
10 am
11 am
NOON

SATURDAY 2

SUNDAY 3

Motivation for the Week

"Action expresses priorities."
— Mahatma Gandhi

DEC 28-31; JAN 1-3
2021

PRINCIPLE OF THE WEEK:

Roles: Personal

ACTION ITEMS

TO DO

28 MONDAY

6 am
7 am
8 am
9 am
10 am
11 am
NOON

1 pm
2 pm
3 pm
4 pm
5 pm
6 pm
7 pm
8 pm

29 TUESDAY

6 am
7 am
8 am
9 am
10 am
11 am
NOON

1 pm
2 pm
3 pm
4 pm
5 pm
6 pm
7 pm
8 pm

30 WEDNESDAY

6 am
7 am
8 am
9 am
10 am
11 am
NOON

1 pm
2 pm
3 pm
4 pm
5 pm
6 pm
7 pm
8 pm

Figure 19. A completed pre-week planning example

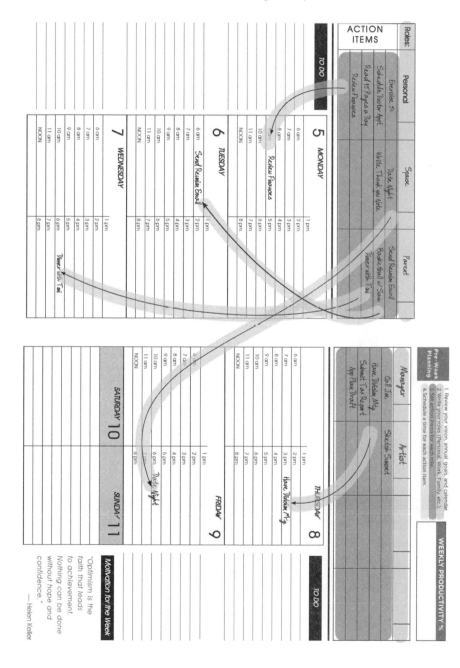

Step 1. Review Your Vision, Roles and Goals, and Long-Range Calendar

Take a few minutes to review your vision and goals; then ask yourself what you can do this week to move toward accomplishing your goals. This review of your vision and goals means you are looking at them at least one time per week—this puts you in an elite statistical number of people.

For some goals, you may have nothing to do this week. For others, it is important that you do specific things this week. For example, maybe one of your goals in the role of parent is to *Hold a family reunion by October 1st*. When you are doing your pre-week planning, you may not need to do anything this week as it relates to that goal. However, if it's April, maybe this week is the time when you need to take certain steps toward accomplishing that goal. Maybe one of your action items is to send out an RSVP email to all family members along with a draft itinerary for the reunion.

Can you see how that simple example moved someone from potentially being in Q1, if they were to procrastinate, to being well ahead of the curve in Q2? It was important to have the goal in the first place, but it is the pre-week planning that helps you connect the action items to accomplishing the goal. When it comes to this particular goal, you won't be doing something *every* week toward accomplishing it. Other goals, such as health goals or sales goals, however, might require you to do something *every* week. That is why the first part of Step 1 is to begin with the vision and goals.

There is a section in the front of our weekly planner in which you can write your vision and goals. We designed the weekly planner to be a one-stop shop so that you can easily and quickly reference your vision and goals each week. For those who do your pre-week planning on the computer, it is essential to have your vision and goals in a place where you can see them every week.

As we mentioned earlier, pre-week planning is a process that can stand on its own and still dramatically increase performance and productivity; however, it is so much more powerful when your daily and weekly actions align with your longer-term vision and goals.

Finally, as part of Step 1, we recommend briefly reviewing your long-term calendar; doing so helps you stay in Q2. For example, it is usually better to book a flight well ahead of time so that you get the flight you want, at a better rate, and with the seat of your choice. The Q2 approach is much better than the alternative of waiting until the day before your trip (Q1), paying for a more expensive ticket, and having your seat options limited.

Step 2. Write Down Your Roles

Just as you did for your vision and goals, identify the five to seven roles that matter most to you. This approach helps you plan your week through the lens of what matters most in each role. Planning your week through the lens of roles is one of the primary differences between this planning process and every other planning process.

Figure 20 shows some potential roles someone might have.

Figure 20. Write your roles

Roles:	Personal	Spouse	Parent	Manager	Artist

Even if you are using an electronic calendar (Google, Outlook, etc.), it is critical that you do these next steps on a piece of paper. We have had conversations with several leading neuroscientists in the world, and all agree that the act of writing unlocks a part of the brain that otherwise stays dormant—when you type, you cannot access it.

If you are using our weekly planner, write your roles across the top in the gray row. You will notice that the personal role is prewritten for you—as we mentioned earlier, this is the most crucial role. In the personal role, you will think about yourself through the lens of what you can do this week to take care of yourself physically, mentally, emotionally, and spiritually. In other words, the personal role is all about you taking care of *you* this week.

In Greek, there are two terms used to think about time: Kairos and Chronos. *Kairos* focuses on priorities (roles), and *Chronos* is all about time. Most planners are focused only on time (Chronos). Pre-week planning brings Kairos and Chronos together so you focus on both your priorities and time. Pre-week planning—looking at your week through the lens of your different roles—is what allows you to lead a life by design, schedule your priorities, and do what matters most. For a lot of people, this approach of using roles is a big shift, because looking at more than just their professional role is new to them.

Step 3. Set Action Items for Each Role

Whether you call them *action items* or *weekly goals*, the bottom line is that in order to come up with these, you have a personal brainstorm with yourself to determine what matters most this week in each role. Imagine how powerful it is to sit down each weekend for a few minutes and identify specific actions that are important in each role! Step 3 is the most critical step of pre-week planning and can enhance almost anything that you might already be doing when it comes to planning.

Figure 21 shows a sample template with weekly action items or weekly goals filled in for each role.

Figure 21. Set action items for each role

Roles:	Personal		Spouse		Parent		Manager		Artist	
ACTION ITEMS	Exercise 5x		Date Night		Send Reunion Email		Call Joe		Sketch Sunset	
	Schedule Doctor Appt		Write Thank you Note		Basketball w/ Sam		Have Division Mtg			
	Read 15 Pages a Day				Dinner with Toni		Submit Tax Report			
	Review Finances						App Plan Draft			

It is this step that moves the majority of your time and focus into Q2. To use the earlier example of ping pong balls, you determine what you should put in the aquarium first—what matters most to you in each role. From the earlier archer example, Step 3 is the equivalent of identifying your bullseye in each role for the week. (We have placed the visuals for these earlier examples here for your convenience; see Figures 22 and 23.)

Figure 22. The ping pong ball example

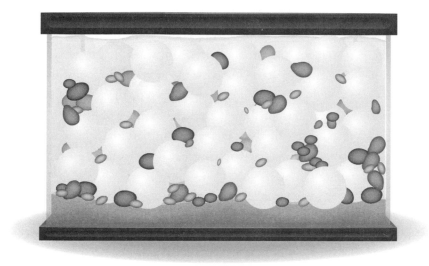

Figure 23. The bullseye example

Pre-week planning is dynamic; every week is likely to be different from the last. Each week, you are apt to have a different number of action items in each role. If you recall, the graph from the previous chapter tracks the average person over five weeks. This person would consistently see a dramatic increase in performance and productivity from week one to week four. In other words, it is okay to start slowly, with only a couple of action items per role. Once you do pre-week planning for two or three weeks, however, you're likely to have additional ideas, and the number of action items you write down in each role will likely increase. This pattern of increasing ideas is why performance and productivity rise when someone consistently does pre-week planning.

You do not need a set number of action items per role. Maybe in the role of spouse, you only have two action items this week, but they are two high-priority weekly goals or action items such as *date night* or *writing a love note*. At the same time, you may have eight or nine specific action items in your professional role that you also consider to be high-priority items. Your filter should be the *do what matters most* filter. Ask yourself if what you write are the Q2 types of activities and ideas.

The following are examples of hypothetical weekly actions by some of the most common roles (these are just examples, and they would not all be done in the same week):

Personal: Run three times, complete two cross-training workouts, do yoga twice, read five chapters of *Start with the Vision*, meditate twice, schedule a physical exam, enroll in an online course, sign up for the September 5k, and so on.

Manager: Take a team member to lunch, finish Part 1 of the strategic plan for our division, do a continue–start–stop with the team, finalize the analytics report for last month, send a birthday note to *X* (a key client), review the purchasing order, schedule one-on-one coaching with (name), and so on.

Spouse or partner: Plan a date night, write a note, send flowers, go on a hike together, make the bed, change the tires, get a new chair that they requested, get the airline tickets for our vacation, and so on.

Parent: Date night with (insert name), go on a bike ride, help build a fort, write a note, get ice cream, play basketball, conduct a one-on-one interview, review roles and goals, call (insert name), and so on.

You can see that although each of these action items seems simple, they can combine to transform a person's life. Think about when John (from PepsiCo) decided to call his son; that seemingly simple action mended a broken relationship and transformed his life!

The real power of pre-week planning is Step 3; that is why the act of writing action items in each role is so important. It is this weekly brainstorm you have with yourself—by role—that is transformational.

Step 4. Schedule a Time for Each Action Item

After you've got your action items planned by role, it's time to make things more concrete. As you can see in Figure 24, you can assign a time for each action item.

Whether you use our weekly planner or an electronic calendar, it is in this step that you assign a time for each action item.

Let's return to the previous parent role example. If you plan to send a reunion RSVP via email to your family, figure out a day and time when you will do it this week. In Figure 24, we assigned that action item to Tuesday at 6 a.m. Likewise, let's say that in the manager role, you plan to meet with one of your team members, finish your strategic plan for your division, call an important client, and conduct a feedback session. When will you do all of these this week?

The point is that you need to assign every action item you come up with in Step 3 a time for when you plan to do it.

• • • •

To reiterate, these are the four simple steps to effectively do pre-week planning: review your vision/goals, identify your roles, determine what matters most in each role this week, and assign a time to each action item. You can

Figure 24. Schedule a time for each action item.

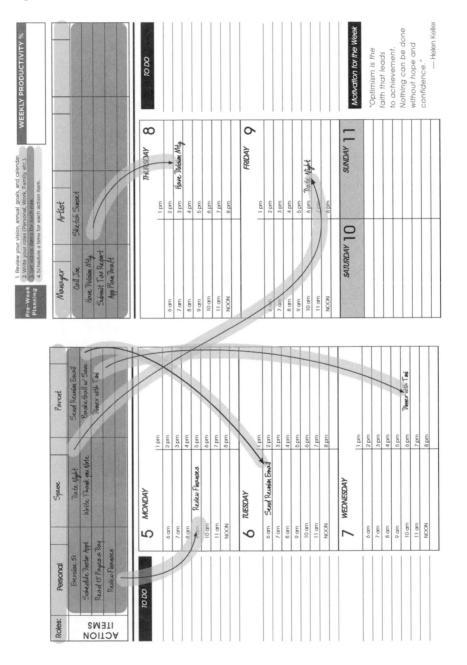

incorporate thousands of variations into pre-week planning, but it is important to keep these four steps as the core process. That is what differentiates this process from every other planning process in the world.

For those of you who would like to track your own progress and stay accountable, we have created a very simple way to do that. In the upper right corner of our planner, you can track the total activities you have planned during the week divided by the total number you have accomplished. This gives you what we call your *productivity quotient*. Ideally, a productivity quotient is in the 70 to 80 percent range. If it dips down to 70 percent or lower, then you need to investigate why. Are you overscheduling, not leaving room for Q1 flexibility, procrastinating? The productivity quotient is one more optional way to hold yourself accountable and measure your productivity.

Take Action

An orthopedic surgeon and successful businessman wisely said that pre-week planning is *simple, but not easy!* What he reiterated is that the process of pre-week planning is simple, but the habit of doing it every week can be challenging. Pre-week planning takes a serious commitment for each of us to set aside the required time each weekend. The weeks when this surgeon does his pre-week planning? Highly productive. The weeks he does not? Higher stress and significantly less productive.

He is not alone in recognizing that this is not an easy habit to develop. Any time a person develops a new habit, it can be challenging, even when the habit itself is powerful. This particular habit requires discipline, which we define as *doing the right thing at the right time regardless of how we feel about it*. When done consistently, it is the sum total of each small action in our roles that transforms our personal and professional lives!

The best time to start pre-week planning is right now—this week! We invite you to pause what you're doing and plan for the remainder of this week. Pull out a sheet of paper or your BYB planner, write down your roles, brainstorm your priorities by role for the remainder of this week, and schedule a time for each one. Go through the four steps right now so you can experience how simple it is.

Then, choose a time this weekend when you are most likely to have some quiet time to do your pre-week planning for the next week. If you have not already done it, set a reminder on your phone for the scheduled time. Some people find it helpful to treat pre-week planning as an ongoing process throughout the weekend. In other words, they start on Friday afternoon before they leave work and add additional actions or ideas to their roles throughout the weekend when they think of them. You can ultimately do whatever works best for you.

Dorene, the COO of Discover Healing, treats it as an ongoing process throughout the weekend and says this about how she does pre-week planning:

> Often, I hear employees speak about the dread of a Monday, and I too have considered that at different times. You know the lyrics "Monday, Monday, can't trust that day. Monday, Monday, sometimes it just turns out that way."
>
> There is an answer to those Monday morning blues. It's called pre-week planning. How refreshing not to have to think about or decide what you have to do first thing Monday morning. With pre-week planning, your week is laid out in front of you, and you know exactly your direction.
>
> I have used pre-week planning for years. On Friday afternoon, I start to plan my next week. Using my planner, I place all my meetings that are recurring for each week. I also arrange any other meetings I know I need to have so that the times are set and coordinated. I take the time to think through the various items I need to accomplish based on my different roles and place those in my plan.
>
> This provides a great start to a great week. My mind doesn't feel overwhelmed because I've already thought through these items and know there is a time for each one.
>
> With pre-week planning, I can think "Monday, Monday, so good to me. Monday mornin', it was all I hoped it would be."

Dorene exemplifies the peace, calm, and focus that accompanies someone who does their pre-week planning and is prepared for a great week—no matter what may show up. She experiences the characteristics that are commonly associated with Q2 versus the stress and crisis-response feelings associated with Q1.

Now that we have seen how well this process works for Dorene, it is time to think about one other idea that has proven valuable—sharing your week with your partner or spouse. One of the primary reasons for divorce or for employees to leave an organization is *frustration*. If you think about the root cause of frustration, it typically stems from misaligned expectations. An employee thinks the leader should be doing Y, and the leader thinks the employee should be doing Y. When those expectations are not aligned, it results in frustration. The same idea is true in relationships. Pre-week planning can help you avoid the inevitable conflicts found in Q1 such as, "I thought *you* were going to take her to soccer!" When you sit down with your partner (hopefully after you have both individually done your own pre-week planning) and align your priorities for the week, it ensures you are going the same direction and that you are focused jointly on what matters most. Most importantly, it aligns expectations and gives clarity for the week!

When Things Do Not Go as Planned

At this point, some people may be thinking, "This all sounds great, but what about when things do not go as planned?" It is a great question, and that is exactly what will happen almost every week!

Remember, the Do What Matters Most matrix from earlier in the book? Look at it again (see Figure 25) and think about how the big three will help someone move the *majority* of their focus to Q2.

In Chapter 2, we mentioned that the optimal high-performance and productivity balance for a person or team is to spend 20 to 25 percent of their time doing Q1 activities, 60 to 70 percent of their time focusing on Q2 activities, 5 to 15 percent of their time managing Q3 activities, and less than 5 percent in Q4 activities. This varies somewhat by industry but holds true in most industries.

As a reminder, the same research showed organizations that struggle, and are far less productive, spend 40 to 50 percent of their time in Q1, 15 to 20 percent of their time in Q2, 30 to 40 percent of their time in Q3, and 10 to 15 percent in Q4.

Figure 25. The Do What Matters Most matrix

	URGENT	**NOT URGENT**
IMPORTANT	**Q1** **DO IT!** High stress, high-priority **EXAMPLES** Crises, emergency meetings, client concerns, pressing problems, deadlines, fires, emergencies	**Q2** **FOCUS** Low stress, high-priority **EXAMPLES** Roles and goals, pre-week planning, weekly alignment meeting, relationship building, exercise, strategic planning, personal or team development
NOT IMPORTANT	**Q3** **MANAGE** Urgent, not important **EXAMPLES** Some email or mail, unnecessary meetings or reports, interruptions, unannounced calls or visits	**Q4** **ELIMINATE** Not urgent, not important **EXAMPLES** Some TV, surfing the internet, wasted time, mindless activities

The point is that Q1 activities will *always* come up during the week. However, when you have developed the habit of pre-week planning, the difference is that you are able to be calm and focused during the storm.

Pre-week planning is a powerful way to reduce stress and increase productivity in each area of your life. It is what also prevents the things that matter most from slipping through the cracks. Of course, things will come up during the week that are urgent and important. No problem! When you have planned your priorities into the week, you can simply ask which is more important, the urgent issue, or what you previously scheduled? If the answer is that the urgent issue is more important, you can simply shift your previously scheduled item to another time. That is low stress, and you are still doing what matters most! The originally planned item will still get done, just not at the originally scheduled time.

For example, imagine you are a website developer, and as part of your pre-week planning, you have decided to test the new website on Tuesday morning. In the middle of this testing, your boss comes in and gives you an urgent project that needs to be completed within the next hour. If the requested project from the boss is urgent (Q1), then you can simply shift the website testing to later in the day and focus on completing the requested project. The point is that the website testing still happens because it is important; it just happens at a different time than originally planned. The result is that you are a team member who is still in Q2 and can handle the Q1 tasks from your supervisor. The whole idea is that when Q1 tasks come up, your previously scheduled priorities can often shift around rather than not get done at all.

It is also important to set the right expectation for yourself. In the previous chapter, we indicated that 70 to 80 percent is the right accomplishment target at the end of the week. A 70–80 percent productivity quotient seems to be the right balance between stretching ourselves and not overscheduling. Give yourself permission right now to *not* accomplish *every* item you planned in the week. If it is important, and you did not accomplish it this week, roll it forward to the next week. Again, it will still get done, just not in the exact timeframe you had originally planned. If you have rolled the same action forward week after week and you are still not doing it, there is likely another reason why it is not getting done.

Lastly, since you know Q1 fires will show up during the week, it is important to be flexible and leave open space in your calendar to move things into if needed. If a person pre-plans every minute of the week into their calendar, then there is very little room for flexibility. That person is setting themselves up not to accomplish several of those planned activities during the week. So, leave some open space and plan for the unexpected.

Wrap Up

Nobody has ever said to us, "Pre-week planning didn't really work for me." Instead, people are always sharing stories about how pre-week planning shifted their focus and helped them accomplish things they had been thinking about for years.

We continue to use the term *life-changing* because we believe pre-week planning is exactly that. How can pre-week planning not be life-changing when a person sits down every week to review their vision and goals, identify their roles for that week, list what matters most in each role, and then assign a time to each item?

Pre-week planning is a habit that takes discipline and consistency, doing it week after week, even when you may not feel like it. When a person has that discipline and is consistent, the rewards are worth it.

Imagine how great it would feel to enjoy your work; be a better contributor; have improved health, relationships, and finances; and have less stress, and a strong sense of purpose and direction. Imagine the team dynamic and how great it would be to have an aligned team focused on Q2 activities, increased profitability, increased productivity, and a fun culture to top it off.

At the beginning of the book, we said doing what matters most is both a *mindset* and a *skillset*. Vision, roles and goals, and pre-week planning are the skillset. The mindset is having the willingness and discipline to consistently apply the skillset.

In the next and final chapter, we want to come back to time and why these habits are so important to start *now*. In addition, we will share a few things that you can consider adding to your vision, goals, and pre-week planning to truly make the most of each day—in other words, to make each day count!

REFLECTION QUESTIONS FOR THIS CHAPTER:

1. How do you feel pre-week planning can help you prioritize your time and do what matters most?

2. Who else do you know who would benefit from doing pre-week planning (son/daughter, partner, team member)? Why would pre-week planning be helpful to them?

3. When do you think is the best time for you to do pre-week planning each week? Have you set an alarm or reminder?

4. Is there someone who you would feel comfortable having as an accountability partner to join you in pre-week planning (co-worker, partner, etc.)?

9

Time and Habits—
Make Each Day Count!

Whee call time the great equalizer because it is the universal resource—we all have access to it, and we all have the same amount of it. What a person does with that time determines their legacy.

To show how important it is to use our time wisely, we want to share a great story we once heard. Since we first heard this story, we have found different versions of it, but it is the principle of the story that is important.

• • • •

One evening a father was trying to finish several important projects with looming deadlines. He had already missed dinner and knew he would be working late into the night. He sat at the kitchen table, in the dimly lit kitchen, sorting through the different charts on his laptop.

His young son approached him and quietly asked his father, "Dad, how much do you make in an hour?" The father felt his frustration start to rise, adding to the stress he already felt from the looming deadlines. This was not the conversation he wanted to be having when he was so focused. He tersely told his young son, "I make about $40 an hour, but that isn't your business." The son then paused and asked his father, "Dad, can I borrow $20?" The dad's patience was gone; he thought his son wanted to buy another toy, and he felt like this conversation was wasting his valuable time. He raised his voice and told his son, "No, I'm not giving you $20; now go to your room!" The dejected young boy lowered his head and quietly walked to his bedroom. The father sat in his chair and fumed. The more he thought about it, the angrier he became.

Then, after about thirty minutes, the father began to calm down, and he realized that he had taken his work frustration out on his young son. His heart softened, and he realized he had been too hard on him. He got up from the table and walked to his son's bedroom. He could hear his son quietly crying as he approached the bedroom, causing his heart to sink even further.

He gently approached his son and sat down next to him on his bed. He said to his son, "I'm sorry that I was so hard on you. It has been a long day, and I took out some of my frustrations on you. You must have had a good reason for wanting the $20. If you need $20, I can give you the $20." His father then handed his son a $20 bill.

His son instantly smiled and wiped away his tears. He sat up in bed and reached over to his bedstand. He anxiously grabbed several more dollar bills that had been sitting there. He quickly counted the money, including the new $20 addition, and saw that he had more than $50. With a big smile, the boy said to his dad, "Dad, I didn't have enough money before, but now I do." He went on to say, "Now that I have $40, can I buy an hour of your time so that we can play together?"

The father was ashamed. His heart sank. He put his arms around his son, feeling his own tears streak down his cheeks. He begged his young son for forgiveness.

• • • •

When we first heard this story, it really touched us. It reminded us that time is fleeting and the time to do what matters most is now. Tomorrow is not guaranteed for anyone. Time is the great equalizer. We all have the same amount of it, and once it is gone, it is gone. It is important to be aware of the destination while still being able to live in the present and enjoy the journey. When people are at work, they should be fully present, engaged, and do what matters most. Then, when they go home, they should be fully present with their partner, children, and even with themselves. Although nobody can be "on" 100 percent of the time, a vision, goals, and pre-week planning help a person accomplish *a lot* more than they likely would otherwise, both at home and at work.

Life is filled with ups and downs as well as unplanned surprises. This inability to predict the future is why the habit of developing your vision and goals and being consistent with pre-week planning is so helpful.

Even when a person is doing all the right things, the unexpected challenges of life will still show up. When you have a clear vision and goals and are consistent with pre-week planning, you will almost always be in a much better position to handle whatever comes your way than someone who does not have this foundation.

For example, we have a dear friend and coaching client, who we will call Nathan. He is an executive of a large, nationally recognized bank. One day, as he was driving with his wife to their cabin, his tire unexpectedly blew out, he lost control, and their SUV rolled several times. Tragically, his wife sustained a head injury and ended up in a coma for nearly 18 months.

Nathan spent many sleepless nights during those 18 months thinking about his life, his work, and his family. This type of accident is not something anyone would wish for, yet Nathan knew he could not go back and change time; he accepted that it did happen, and that it could happen to anyone. Nearly everything in his life was going great before the accident. However, by the end of that tragic day, his life was flipped upside down.

During this challenging time, Nathan was still an executive at the bank, he was still a father to several adult children, and he was still a grandparent to several grandchildren. He still needed to "show up" and be there for his team, his family, and even for himself. When he went back to his vision, goals, and what he could focus on each week that mattered most (pre-week planning), that is what kept him from going to a dark place.

During this time, Nathan made a concerted effort to stay focused on his vision (his purpose), his goals, and what mattered most each week. He used his time to focus on what he could control rather than on what he could not. He visited his wife every day in the hospital to talk with her and caress her hand, even though she could not respond—he stayed connected. He spent time with his children, he was a more committed leader at the bank, and he took a more profound interest in his team and clients. This grueling period was a time of deep introspection for Nathan. After 18 months, and many consultations with the doctors, the family finally made the agonizing decision to end her life-support.

Nathan's vision, goals, and pre-week planning took an ugly situation that nobody would ever wish for and helped him make the best of it. He believes that there is a higher power, and he used this experience to become a better version of himself, a better leader, a better father, grandfather, and community member. The people on Nathan's team expressed that he is one of the best leaders they have ever worked with throughout their careers, and this experience made him a better leader than he already was.

As was the case with Nathan, no matter what may come your way, when you have the big three, you are in a stronger position to handle whatever is thrown at you—big or small. These three habits give you a reason to get up every morning; they give your heart a reason to keep beating. They help you stay tuned in to what you can control instead of worrying about what you cannot. They help you be one of the best contributors to your team. And finally, they help you focus on what matters most with the precious time you have.

Habits

Ultimately, what the big three will do is help you develop great habits and sustain momentum. You will see an immediate impact on performance and productivity at both personal and professional levels. One of the most critical personal commitments to make is to commit to the habit of pre-week planning. Pre-week planning is the single habit that aligns your actions with your vision and goals.

Although a team can undoubtedly apply this skillset collectively, the real power comes when individuals make internal commitments to themselves. These commitments come from within, and once started, can transform small sparks into roaring flames.

Maintaining the habit of pre-week planning and staying connected to your vision and goals takes discipline. You need to decide, and decide now, how committed you are to doing what matters most. Life is about choices and habits. For example, if you decide to live in Europe, that decision becomes a big part of your life. If you decide to change jobs, that too affects your life. When you decide and make a choice, the rest of your life is affected.

Decisions are one of life's crossroads that have ramifications for the rest of your life. If you decide to commit to pre-week planning and want assistance with accountability, then get a coach. You can also enlist a partner or coworker to help with accountability and return the favor if they ask. The point is that once you make a decision to do the big three, it will positively affect your life in many ways.

Your life, and your impact on the world, is the sum of your habits! So, each of us better be vigilant about what habits we choose to form.

One of our favorite poems, from an unknown author, illustrates the undeniable power of our habits:

I am your constant companion.
I am your greatest helper or your heaviest burden.
I will push you onward or drag you down to failure.
I am completely at your command.

Half the things you do, you might just as well turn over to me,
and I will do them quickly and correctly.
I am easily managed; but, you must be firm with me.
Show me exactly how you want something done, and after
a few lessons I will do it automatically.

I am the servant of all great people.
And, alas, of all failures as well.
Those who are great, I have made great.
Those who are failures, I have made failures.
I am not a machine, though I work with the precision of a machine.
Plus, the intelligence of a person.

You may run me for profit, or run me for ruin; it makes
no difference to me.
Take me, train me, be firm with me and I will place
the world at your feet.
Be easy with me, and I will destroy you.
Who am I?

I AM HABIT!

Isn't that a great poem? It makes us introspectively look at each one of our habits and ask whether they are moving us toward our vision or away from it.

Most of us have areas of our lives we want to improve, whether it is making more money, obtaining a promotion, improving a specific relationship, or achieving improved health. In most cases, our daily habits determine how we do in each of those areas. If you want to improve an area of your life, doing so starts with the development of the vision, identifying specific goals for that area, and then being disciplined about what you will do each week in that area.

In other words, we need to develop the habits that lead toward achieving our vision and goals.

Speaking of habits, when executives, managers, and employees share their concerns about what keeps them up at night or what consumes a lot of their thoughts, several recurring themes surface:

1. Personal health and well-being

2. Relationships

3. Money

4. Connecting with a purpose

5. Doing something they enjoy

6. Job performance

Although there could be an endless list of concerns, these six tend to be the ones that show up the most. This is why the big three become so important; they help a person develop the right habits and focus on these key subjects. The big three help a person improve every one of these areas when the person is consistent and disciplined.

Now that you have read the chapters about vision, goals, and pre-week planning, look at your own life and ask a few thoughtful questions related to your current habits:

1. *What do I want to improve about my habits related to my health, diet, and exercise?*

2. *What do I want to improve in my relationships with my partner, children, clients, and coworkers?*

3. *How can I improve my finances to include minimizing debt, saving, and developing a plan for my long-term financial goals?*

4. *What can I do to be happier so that when I wake up, I am excited for the day?*

5. *How can I be a more productive member of my organization? If applicable, how can I improve as a leader to inspire my team and help them achieve their fullest potential?*

Answering these questions is simply a place to start to help you think in terms of what matters most. Indeed, if you take just a couple of minutes to ponder these questions, you will get some ideas of areas you would like to improve. Maybe you can take some of your internal answers to those questions and make them a part of your vision and goals.

The habits that you work to develop in the coming weeks, months, and years will ultimately help you achieve what you want to accomplish. If a person wants to improve something in their life, there is usually a corresponding habit that needs to be adjusted or developed. In some cases, that means you develop new and helpful habits, and in other cases, you change old and unhelpful habits. In other words, your habits move you either toward or away from your vision and goals.

The big three increase performance and productivity while transforming lives by helping us develop new habits. Think about the impact the big three had on our CEO friend from South Africa who laid down his last pack of cigarettes; the sales team that went from averaging 17 to 34 sales a day; John, the PepsiCo executive who rekindled a relationship with his son; or Jill, who went from being a mediocre employee to one of the top performers on the team! You get the idea. Vision, goals, and pre-week planning are about creating high-performance habits that align your time and energy to what matters most.

The first step toward developing successful habits is to identify what your vision and goals are. Then, pre-week planning helps you use your time at the daily and weekly level to develop those habits and consistently achieve your vision and goals.

Supercharged Productivity Tips

When we decided to write this book, we purposefully chose to focus exclusively on the big three. After all, they alone will help someone do what only 1 percent of people have done. They will increase productivity by an average of *at least* 30 to 50 percent and have a significant impact on the performance and productivity of your team members. Although the entire focus of the book has been on the big three, we also want to share a small handful of productivity tips that are also important. Based on the other findings in our research, we felt these tips would be helpful to include because you can implement them in conjunction with the big three. Remember, these additional tips are just that . . . tips. We want the focus to stay on the big three but feel that a brief summary of these five tips will also increase productivity and help maximize your time.

1. Becoming Your Best morning routine

The morning sets the tone for the day, and the day usually goes better when we get off to a strong start. Including the following list of things as part of your pre-week planning will help you get off to a great start in the morning. To be clear, we are not suggesting you do *all* of these things each day; instead, choose what matters most and plan them into your week as part of your pre-week planning:

- Get seven to eight hours of sleep.

- Immediately drink 16+ ounces of water each morning when you wake up.
- Make your bed.
- Stretch; take a few minutes for some form of yoga or meditation.
- Exercise.
- Meditate.
- Ask yourself what you can do to make it a great day.
- Take three to four minutes before you roll out of bed to focus on your vision or positive affirmations. What will you do today to make them a reality?
- Review the key actions and calendar for the day. Identify the top one or two priorities for the day.

When possible, *do not* look at your phone or email for the first 30 minutes of the day. Use that time to focus on you and your personal role. You will find that it is quite common to have more energy throughout the day when you take care of yourself first.

2. Sleep, exercise, and a healthy diet

Countless books have been written on each one of these. Suffice it to say that a person who sleeps well, makes time to exercise, and is conscious of the food they eat will likely perform and produce at a higher level than someone who does not. Also, these three things contribute to your longevity and increased happiness. If you have not incorporated aspects of sleep, exercise, and diet into your vision and goals, we highly recommend you consider doing so.

Our bodies are like jets. You cannot put water into the fuel tank of a jet and expect it to perform well—a jet needs jet fuel. Likewise, our bodies need "fuel" to perform well, and that often comes in the form of sleep, exercise, and the food we eat.

One of the keys to getting the right amount of sleep, the right amount of exercise, and a proper diet is what you intentionally plan into your week during pre-week planning.

3. *Chairfly your day.*

You're probably wondering what *chairfly* means. The most successful pilots are the ones who chairfly the important parts of their mission before they fly it. In other words, before they walk out to the jet, the pilots visualize the most critical aspects of the upcoming flight in their mind's eye. In the calm of the briefing room, they mentally walk through (visualize) the busiest, most intense parts of their flight *before* they get in their jets and execute it in the air.

Likewise, we invite you to take a few minutes in the morning to chairfly your day.

To chairfly, sit down and review your calendar. Review what you scheduled for the day as part of your pre-week planning and identify the two or three highest priorities. When possible, it often helps to schedule the highest priority items in the morning, when your energy level is high. We recognize that this is not always possible, but when you can, the morning is usually the ideal time to get things done.

Once you identify the two or three priorities for the day, you can calmly close your eyes and chairfly your day. Mentally walk through it and get prepared for what might show up unannounced. This way, if a Q1 item pops up, you know what your priorities are and how you might shift things around.

Instead of just jumping into the day and blindly hoping for the best, take a couple of minutes to chairfly—you will feel calmer, more focused, and at peace with your day.

4. *Improve your workstation with multiple monitors.*

You can accomplish a lot with just one monitor, but two or more monitors will allow you to accomplish the same task in a fraction of the time. In the *New York Times* report of a Jon Peddie Research survey, dual monitors proved to increase productivity by up to 46 percent.[22]

You can find the number of monitors that work best for you. Everyone we have talked with agrees that when you have multiple monitors, you can get work done more effectively and efficiently. For example, Rob uses four monitors, and he can get done in about 20 to 30 minutes what used to take him an hour to do with just one screen.

5. Learn to say no.

If a coworker or peer is continually asking you to do things that put you in Q1 or Q3, it almost always has a significant impact on your productivity. Being able to say *no*, the right way, is beneficial to the entire team. For example, if a boss comes to you and asks you to take care of a project while you are in the middle of another project, it is crucial to base your decision of what to do on what is best for you, your boss, and the company. One example of a good response is to say, "Yes, I can work on this project (the new one), but I'll need to stop working on X to finish this new project. That means I will not be able to have X done by the time I promised. Would you prefer I finish the other project on time or work on this new project?" This type of statement puts the ball in the court of the supervisor and is often received very well. It aligns expectations and helps the supervisor understand what you are already working on. If the new project is more important, the supervisor will likely be okay with the other project being late. If the other project being on time is more important, then the supervisor is aware of that.

The ability to say *no* is undoubtedly an art. The whole point of this book is to help you do what matters most. Sometimes, that means people need to unload certain commitments so that they can use their time to refocus on their priorities.

Wrap Up

Time is our most valuable resource. Life is about the journey as much as it is about the destination. The whole point in having a vision, establishing roles and goals, and doing pre-week planning is to learn to live in the present while having an eye on the future. Ultimately, what you do with your time will form your habits, and your habits will define your legacy. The vision is your internal compass, the roles and goals are your annual targets, and pre-week planning is about living in the present to make each day count!

The big three are life-changing habits and will have an enormous impact on both performance and productivity. Like anything, you will require discipline and focus to ingrain these habits in your life. We invite you to make an internal commitment and join us in making the big three lifelong habits.

W. Clement Stone, a businessman, philanthropist, and author, wisely said, "I think there is something more important than believing: Action! The world is full of dreamers, and there aren't enough who will move ahead and begin to take concrete steps to actualize their vision."

When you are considering your life, taking action to stay focused on the big three may be one of the most important things you ever do!

One of the most common questions we get after someone has started on their vision, goals, and pre-week planning is, "What now?" In the conclusion, we will answer this question and share some additional ways to sustain the momentum!

REFLECTION QUESTIONS FOR THIS CHAPTER:

1. What is one area of your life you would like to commit more time and effort to?

2. What is one habit you would like to develop, change, or stop?

3. While you read this chapter, what are some thoughts that came to your mind regarding your own life (both personal and professional)?

4. Is there someone who you can discuss this chapter with to explore time, habits, and what matters most?

5. How can the combination of your vision, roles and goals, and pre-week planning empower you to do what matters most?

CONCLUSION

What Now?

In the beginning, we promised that the big three would increase your performance and productivity by at least 30 to 50 percent. Now that you have read the book, can you see and feel how powerful the big three are?

Let us get more specific in terms of what this can mean for you. In Chapter 7, we illustrated how someone doing pre-week planning accomplished an average of 20 to 30 more activities/tasks during the week (with less stress) than someone who did not do pre-week planning. Over a month, that equates to an additional 80 to 120 activities. In a year, that equates to an additional 900 to 1,400 activities.

Imagine the cumulative impact of maintaining these three habits for the rest of your life. Over 40 years, that equates to an additional 30,000 to 40,000+ activities that likely would not have been accomplished without these habits!

On paper, those are numbers. Yet, every one of those numbers represents a meaningful activity in your life. It could represent an exercise, a gesture of kindness to your spouse, an important activity related to your job, taking care of something for a client or team member, or something you do for a son or daughter. The point is, every one of those numbers represents something important to you.

The beauty of the whole thing is that while a person is doing what matters most and accomplishing more, stress and task saturation decrease. In other words, peace increases, productivity increases, and stress decreases.

Steve's Journey

None of us know how long we will have in this journey of life, but whatever time we have, we will likely look back and say, "It passed us by as if it were a dream." To illustrate this point, we will share one final and personal example from Steve's life. At the young age of 55, Steve's wife, Roxanne (Rob's mother), was diagnosed with early-onset Alzheimer's disease. This diagnosis was unexpected and suddenly changed nearly all their long-term plans. You can certainly imagine how you would feel if your lifelong partner was given a final sentence that would change every one of your "golden year" plans. Early-onset Alzheimer's is a terminal disease that usually takes the person's life within about ten years from the time of the diagnosis.

Sure enough, at the time of this writing, it has been about ten years since Roxanne's diagnosis. During the past ten years, the decline in her cognitive skills and functionality has been slow and steady. At this point, she is in a care center, can barely utter a word, does not recognize her family, and is wholly dependent on others for food and care. It has been a difficult and challenging process to watch the slow degradation of such an amazing woman to one who is now entirely dependent on people she does not recognize.

Yet, in this process that nobody ever wished for, I (Rob) have watched my hero father focus on his vision, goals, and pre-week planning. It is the combination of the big three that helped him control what he could control and stay focused on what mattered most.

In the early stages, Roxanne and Steve set new goals to travel the world together and make memories while they could. Roxanne accompanied Steve on many of his speaking engagements and corporate training events.

Through this challenging time, Steve's focus on the big three has helped him stay focused on what matters most. Fast forward to today, and Roxanne continues to be Steve's highest priority. Every night he visits Roxanne in the care center and patiently takes care of her—he treats her like a queen. Even though she no longer recognizes him, he brings her flowers, chocolates, and picture books, and tries to brighten her day in some way.

Part of his new vision is to help her feel comfortable and live the final part of her life with dignity, feeling happy. He strokes her hand and helps her do one of the only things she can do to express herself . . . smile. He often sits with her and reviews picture books they created from their trips and time together. The only benefit to Alzheimer's is that every day is a new day, and they can look at the same pictures as if Roxanne had never seen them before.

The big three are about far more than professional success. In Steve's case, he has balanced his time between running multiple businesses, spending time with his family, and taking care of his beloved wife of more than 45 years. When Roxanne was diagnosed with Alzheimer's, Steve's vision changed. Rather than focus on the negative, Steve adjusted his vision and set new goals. Even today, it is the consistent habit of pre-week planning that helps him stay focused on what he can control and do what matters most.

No matter what curve balls life may throw, the big three will help you make the best of whatever comes your way!

How to Sustain the Momentum

Now that you have finished the book, the most common question is, *What do I do now?*

Here is a list of things you can do to maximize your success and sustain the momentum:

1. **Take or retake the performance and productivity self-assessment found at BYBassessment.com.** If you took it as you started the book, we invite you to retake it *after* you finish your vision and goals and *after* you have been doing pre-week planning for at least one month. A simple way to make sure the retake happens is to schedule it on your long-range calendar right now. We invite you to put it on your calendar for at least one month from now and include the website link. At that point, all you need to do is go the website and take the assessment. Once you do this, compare where you were at the beginning of this book against where you currently are; we are confident you will see a big difference in almost every area of your life!

2. **Finish a draft of your written personal vision as well as your roles and goals.** Once you finish your vision and roles and goals, you

can put them in front of your weekly planner or in a place where you will see them each week when you do pre-week planning. Also, share your vision and goals with a handful of people who you respect and admire. At the end of the year, report back to them on how you did—this will increase accountability.

3. **Commit to doing pre-week planning for an entire year.** Remember, pre-week planning is both a mindset and a skillset. It will require discipline to commit to pre-week planning every week. If you believe the tool of the physical planner would be helpful, you can get your weekly planner when you visit the store at BecomingYourBest.com.

4. **Join the 52-Week Success Rhythm.** The old saying, "Out of sight, out of mind" can be reversed: "Front of sight, front of mind." The success rhythm gives you something to do every day of every week. When you join, we will send you a daily message, story, or quote to keep what matters most in the forefront of your mind. To join the 52-Week Success Rhythm, visit TheSuccessRhythm.com, and start today.

5. **Subscribe to our free weekly podcast.** You can listen to our weekly podcast via iTunes and Stitcher, or you can listen to it when you visit our website at BecomingYourBest.com.

6. **Join our Peak Performance monthly coaching program.** As part of this program, you will join a group of highly motivated people and we will meet every month. The monthly coaching program is a great way to keep moving forward, to add accountability, and to share new research or ideas. We priced this program so that anyone serious about their success can afford it. People appreciate the new ideas, the collaboration, and the accountability that is all part of this program. You can get more details on the homepage located at BecomingYourBest.com by clicking on the drop-down menu in the upper right-hand corner.

These are a few things you can do right now to maximize your success and sustain the momentum!

Wrap Up

Congratulations on finishing the book!

The reality is that this is not the end; it is just the beginning. The art is in the start, and now is the time to start. Developing these habits will be a journey that transforms every area of your personal and professional lives—as it has for us and thousands of others.

We invite you to share this book with your coworkers, friends, and family members so that they too can develop their vision, roles and goals, and the habit of pre-week planning. Additionally, we invite you to share your story by emailing us at Support@BecomingYourBest.com. We would love to hear what the experience was like for you after you develop the big three.

Ella Wheeler Wilcox, a famous author and poet from the late 1800s, shared a thought that applies to each of us:

> *One ship [sails] east and another west, with the selfsame*
> *winds that blow. 'Tis the set of the sail, and not the gale, that*
> *[determines] the way [they'll] go. Like the winds of the sea are*
> *the ways of fate; as we voyage along through life, 'Tis the set of*
> *a soul, that decides its goal, and not the calm or the strife.*[23]

In the spirit of Ella's quote, there is a wind blowing at each of our backs. The question is, How will we each choose to set our sails to catch it?

The big three empowers each of us to hoist and set our sails, catch the wind, and do what matters most!

NOTES

1. Henry Mintzberg, "The Manager's Job: Folklore and Fact," *Harvard Business Review*, March–April 1990, https://hbr.org/1990/03/the-managers-job-folklore-and-fact.

2. Og Mandino, *The Greatest Salesman in the World* (New York: Bantam Books, 1983) 47.

3. *Merriam-Webster*, s.v. "productivity," accessed November 4, 2020, https://www.merriam-webster.com/dictionary/productivity.

4. *Merriam-Webster*, s.v. "performance," accessed November 4, 2020, https://www.merriam-webster.com/dictionary/performance.

5. Jim Harter, "Employee Engagement on the Rise in the U.S.," Gallup, August 26, 2018, https://news.gallup.com/poll/241649/employee-engagement-rise.aspx.

6. David Woods, "Three Quarters of Employees Want More Training at Work to Fulfill Their Full Potential, Middlesex University Reports," *HR Magazine*, May 18, 2011, https://www.hrmagazine.co.uk/article-details/three-quarters-of-employees-want-more-training-at-work-to-fulfill-their-full-potential-middlesex-university-reports.

7. Integra, "IRR Sponsored Study: 'Desk Rage' and Workplace Stress," Integra Realty Resources, November 29, 2000, https://www.irr.com/news/irr-sponsored-study-desk-rage-and-workplace-stress-9677.

8. Harter, "Employee Engagement on Rise."

9. Kermit Pattison, "Worker Interrupted: The Cost of Task Switching," *Fast-Company*, July 28, 2008, https://www.fastcompany.com/944128/worker-interrupted-cost-task-switching.

10. The Radicati Group, "Email Statistics Report 2015–2019," March 2015, 4, http://www.radicati.com/wp/wp-content/uploads/2015/02/Email-Statistics-Report-2015-2019-Executive-Summary.pdf.

11. VitalSmarts, "Is Your Team a Ticking Time Bomb? New Research Shows It Only Takes 1 to 2 Team Members to Undermine Results When They Fumble Tasks and Responsibilities," *Cision PR Newswire*, May 16, 2019, https://www.prnewswire.com/news-releases/is-your-team-a-ticking-time-bomb-new-research-shows-it-only-takes-1-or-2-team-members-to-undermine-results-when-they-fumble-tasks-and-responsibilities-300851400.html.

12. Becoming Your Best Global Leadership, Performance and Productivity Survey, 2018–2019.

13. Source: Becoming Your Best Global Leadership.

14. Becoming Your Best Global Leadership, Performance and Productivity Survey, 2018–2019.

15. Tom Benson, "Re-Living the Wright Way: Biography of Orville Wright," National Aeronautics and Space Administration, last modified June 12, 2014, 05:10, https://wright.nasa.gov/orville.htm.

16. Wikipedia, "Wright Flyer," Wikimedia Foundation, last modified October 23, 2020, 03:22, https://en.wikipedia.org/wiki/Wright_Flyer.

17. Jim Collins, *Good to Great: Why Some Companies Make the Leap and Others Don't* (William Collins, 2001), 42.

18. James Allen, "Visions and Ideals," in *As a Man Thinketh* (Chicago: Sheldon University Press, 1908), 86.

19. Lewis Carroll, *Alice's Adventures in Wonderland*, Chapter 6, last updated October 12, 2020, https://www.gutenberg.org/files/11/11-h/11-h.htm.

20. Shivali Best, "Day That People Most Likely to Give Up Their New Year's Resolutions—And It's Very Soon," *The Mirror*, January 2, 2020, https://www.mirror.co.uk/science/day-people-most-likely-give-21199904.

21. Mandino, *Greatest Salesman in the World*, 67.

22. Jon Peddie Research, "Jon Peddie Research: Multiple Displays Can Increase Productivity by 42%," JPR, October 26, 2017, https://www.jonpeddie.com/press-releases/jon-peddie-research-multiple-displays-can-increase-productivity-by-42/.

23. Ella Wheeler Wilcox, *World Voices* (New York: Hearst's International Library Company, 1916).

DO WHAT MATTERS MOST DISCUSSION GUIDE

We hope the three high-performance habits shared in *Do What Matters Most* have had a significant impact in your life. As you read throughout the book, the promise is that these habits will increase performance and productivity by at least 30 to 50 percent, and more importantly, empower people to prioritize their time and do what matters most!

These discussion questions are meant to summarize the book and should be considered from an individual and team level.

INDIVIDUALS

1. What areas of your personal and professional lives would you like to improve? What is your current mindset toward those areas?

2. How do you currently measure performance and productivity in your life?

3. Using the Do What Matters Most matrix, what quadrant do you spend most of your time in? Why?

4. Because we have all been in different quadrants at different times, how would you describe the emotions associated with each quadrant?

5. What is the difference in feeling between Q2 and every other quadrant?

6. How would a guiding personal vision affect your life for good?

7. What specific area of your life would be most affected by having more direction and focus?

8. There are four questions in the book designed to fire up your imagination *prior* to writing your vision. How would you answer each of these?

    A. In 10 to 20 years, what are some things you want to do and accomplish?

    B. Think of any mentors or people who have inspired you (these can be people you know personally or people you know through history). What are the traits, characteristics, and qualities that you admire about each of these people?

    C. What would you like to improve in your job, your home, or your community?

    D. Fifty years from today, whether you are alive or not, how do you hope others will look back and describe you?

9. What are the five to seven most important roles in your life (personal/ self,* *job title*, parent, spouse/partner, brother/sister, son/daughter, etc.)? *Remember, personal or self is the most important role!

10. What is your vision for each of those roles (the absolute best version of yourself by role)?

11. What was the experience of developing your written personal vision like for you?

12. Where will you put your personal vision so that you can reference it each week as part of pre-week planning?

13. What are one to four SMART goals (by role) for this year that support your vision?

14. What was the experience of developing your roles and goals like for you?

15. Who are three to five people who you could share your goals with to increase accountability?

16. Who else do you know who would benefit from developing their vision and goals?

17. How can pre-week planning help you prioritize your time and do what matters most?

18. When is the best time of the week to allocate 20 to 40 minutes to do pre-week planning? Have you set a reminder on your phone?

19. What is one habit you would like to develop, change, or stop?

20. How can the big three empower you to do what matters most? In other words, how will they improve your life?

TEAM

1. What is the current mindset and culture that exists within your team?

2. How do you measure performance and productivity?

3. What can each team member do to be a better contributor or leader?

4. How can your team be more aligned around a compelling vision?

5. What would be the impact on your team if each person had a written personal vision?

6. Does the personal vision of your team members and coworkers align with their role and the vision of the organization? If so, great. If not, why?

7. How does your team feel about goal setting?

8. How many team members currently have specific, measurable goals for the month, quarter, or year?

9. How often do you or your team review your goals?

10. How can the goals be worded to eliminate such words as *more* or *better*? In other words, how can they be worded in a way that creates a clear target?

11. How are your team members or coworkers prioritizing their time to do what matters most?

12. How can pre-week planning help your team members or coworkers improve their focus on what matters most?

13. If each person reviewed their monthly, quarterly, or annual goals each week as part of pre-week planning, what impact would it have on the team?

14. Is there a team member who you can join up with as an accountability partner to develop the habit of pre-week planning each week?

15. How aligned is your team currently? How could pre-week planning help each individual be more aligned to what matters most?

16. Do you meet weekly as a team to make sure you are aligned? If not, when could you?

17. If you could wave a magic wand and improve one aspect of your team, what would it be?

18. How can the big three help your coworkers or team members increase performance and productivity?

ACKNOWLEDGMENTS

We are deeply grateful to the people who invested so much time and effort to help with the research, editing, and organization of *Do What Matters Most*. We want to highlight some of the people who have been instrumental in helping publish this book.

Thank you to the members of the amazing team at Becoming Your Best who have been with us for years doing a lot of the behind-the-scenes work: Jamie Thorup, Murphy Smith, Quincy Whittaker, Hanna Fabrizio, Carli Sorenson, Tommy Shallenberger, Laura Shallenberger, and Anne Petersen.

Thank you to the incredible team at Berrett-Koehler for your wise counsel, recommendations, and efforts. There were many people involved in the design team, marketing team, and editorial committees. We wanted to especially thank Steve Piersanti, Jeevan Sivasubramaniam, Valerie Caldwell, Rebecca Rider, and Maureen Forys.

To those who provided edits, proofreads, recommendations, and new ideas . . . thank you! Mark Holland, Katie McKnight, Thomas Blackwell, Gary Marlowe, Sue Muehlbach, William Thompson, Kerry Mitchell, Mike Choutka, Melanie Wong, John Jeppson, Suzanne Oliver, Pat Do, Zach Gajewski, Josh Vahovius, Jeff Arnold, Max Ganado, Bruce Matulich, Jean Henri Lhuillier, Terry Grant, Minal Shah, Bobby Gadhia, Noel Otto, Emery Rubagenga, Dan Cantaragiu, Reuben Xuereb, David Xuereb, Charles Spalding, Raul Arizpe, Thibault Relecom, Jody Richards, Erin Galyean, Rick Taylor, Erick McHenry, Jassim Alharoon, Sulaiman Altehaini, Abdulaziz Alahmadi, Abdullah Al-Sharif, and Melanie Gentry.

We also want to acknowledge and thank some of the key mentors and influencers who have had a big impact on our lives: David Clark, Cal Clark, David Conger, Robert Dellenbach, William Jones, Thomas Monson, Stephen Covey, Gardner Russell, Lael Woodbury, and our wonderful friends at Synergy Companies.

For our family members, you have been the backbone and support who give us the ability to work on these kinds of projects. Thank you to Roxanne, David, Steven, Tommy, Daniel, and Anne (and each of their amazing spouses)! In addition, thank you to Tonya, Robbie, Bella, Lana, and Clara. We love every one of you and hope you will share the habits in this book with future generations.

Above all, we want to acknowledge God as the source of inspiration and guidance throughout the years. We believe these principles and habits are divinely inspired and will help people and organizations achieve the very best versions of themselves!

—STEVEN AND ROB SHALLENBERGER

INDEX

ABOUT THE AUTHORS

Rob Shallenberger

Rob has always been intrigued by adventure and had a drive to challenge himself. After graduating from Utah State University and earning an MBA from Colorado State University, he became a fighter pilot in the United States Air Force. During his time in the Air Force, Rob was also an Advance Agent for Air Force One. This was an exciting time because he was able to work with foreign embassies, the secret service, and the White House staff.

As an F-16 pilot and Air Force One Advance Agent, Rob experienced firsthand what a high-performance culture looked like. In that world, the standard is perfection, yet the perfect flight has yet to happen. So, an integral part of the culture was the debrief. In the debrief, the pilots would develop lessons learned to repeat successes and eliminate failures and mistakes. Part of the fighter pilot culture is that when a pilot is tasked with something, they do it right and do it on time. Rob found this high-performance culture fun, exciting, and results-focused. What makes the fighter pilot culture elite are the people and the extensive training that align processes and efforts!

Rob wanted to bring this same high-performance culture to the public and private sector, so it has been the perfect match for him to partner with his father, who had already been researching high-performance for decades. Together, Rob and Steve founded Becoming Your Best Global Leadership and continued the research, which culminated, initially, in the release of their first book, *Becoming Your Best: The 12 Principles of Highly Successful Leaders*. Following the release of *Becoming Your Best*, they went on to author five other books including *Start with the Vision: The Six Steps to Effectively Plan, Create Solutions, and Achieve Your Goals*; *Conquer Anxiety*; and *How to Succeed in High School* (for teenagers and their parents).

Rob considers it an honor to have personally trained hundreds of organizations around the world focused on the 12 principles of highly successful leaders and the big three habits from *Do What Matters Most*. He loves to hear stories about how these habits have transformed lives, both personally and professionally.

Like his father, Rob's primary focus is on his faith and family. He's been married for 23 years and has four children.

Steve Shallenberger

 After graduating from Brigham Young University in accounting, Steve bought his first company at 26 years old. It quickly grew, and before he knew it, the company had more than 700 employees. Many of the employees were sales reps who traveled around the country each summer selling books, videos, and other products.

It was common for the managers or sales reps to ask him, "What principles or habits should I focus on to be among the best?" At the time, Steve had a few ideas, but the more he thought about that question, the more he realized that there had to be a better answer. Thus, he started his journey researching great leaders and high performers to determine what set them apart from everyone else. Identifying the 12 principles of highly successful people and leaders was the culmination of 40 years of research.

Based on that research, Steve and Rob started Becoming Your Best Global Leadership. Their focus is on helping organizations develop high-performing people and teams that know how to focus on what matters most. Becoming Your Best Global Leadership was named one of the top three global leadership programs by HR.com, and it continues to win awards for the high caliber training and impact it is having on performance and productivity.

Steve has had the opportunity to train public and private organizations throughout many parts of the world. He is constantly reminded that while we are diverse in many ways, the foundations of personal and professional success—the big three habits shared in this book—transcend race, culture, and gender.

Throughout his life, Steve has been a part of several organizations that have had a deep impact on him and his research. He graduated from the Harvard Business School Owner/President Management (OPM) program and has been influenced by many of his peers who he continues to associate with decades later. He has also been a part of the Young Presidents Organization (YPO) for more than 38 years; the relationships, adventures, and experiences with YPO have influenced many aspects of Steve's life.

Steve's most important focus has always been his family. He has been married for 46 years and has 6 children and 21 grandchildren.

ABOUT BECOMING YOUR BEST GLOBAL LEADERSHIP

Becoming Your Best Global Leadership is a top-rated leadership training company that is home to a suite of award-winning training solutions. Its training is delivered through both live and virtual keynotes, certification, workshops, and coaching to transform people and empower both public and private organizations to create a culture by design.

Becoming Your Best specializes in the following areas:

1. Leadership
2. Time-management, well-being, and productivity
3. Planning and problem solving
4. Strategic planning and alignment

In 2018, Becoming Your Best won an award for "Best Global Leadership Program" from HR.com for its measured training results and the impact it had in organizations. Our standard is that whether the training is delivered by one of our master trainers or a certified trainer within your organization, productivity and performance will increase by an average of 30 to 50 percent because of our proprietary time-management tools and processes! Those results can be expected from executives, managers, and front-line team members.

Becoming Your Best's first book, *Becoming Your Best: The 12 Principles of Highly Successful Leaders*, is a national bestseller and was founded on 40 years of research to identify what set apart the top 10 percent of great leaders and high performers across industries. Of course, nobody who we researched was perfect (none of us are), but when we saw what high performers focused on, the 12 principles were clearly the common denominator of success among them. Based on the 12 principles, Becoming Your Best established the foundation of its award-winning leadership training and has trained hundreds of public and private organizations around the world.

The next book released was *Start with the Vision: Six Steps to Effectively Plan, Create Solutions, and Take Action.* In our ongoing research, we found that only 10 percent of organizations have a planning or problem-solving process that is used across the team and/or organization. The six-step process brings teams and organizations together with a common language and planning process to address any issue, saving them countless hours and a significant amount of money while fostering imagination and collaboration.

This book—*Do What Matters Most*—will close the time-management and productivity gap that so many people and organizations experience. The Do What Matters Most training and certification is life-changing and empowers team members to focus on three high-performance habits that less than 1 percent of people do!

Companies such as Charles Schwab, PepsiCo, the Dallas Cowboys, and many others have gone through this training with impressive results. In addition to Fortune 500 companies, small start-ups to large government organizations have also experienced how effective the Becoming Your Best training is with their people and teams. We have licensed partners and certified corporate trainers throughout the world, and we are continually expanding into more countries.

Our Vision

The vision for Becoming Your Best Global Leadership is to positively impact a billion lives. Reaching one billion people is an understandably lofty vision that will take years, maybe even decades.

One of the keys to achieving this vision is using content and training that are simple, fun, and scalable and that have a tremendous impact on personal and professional results. In addition, accomplishing this vision will happen exponentially faster when certified trainers take this results-focused training wide and deep throughout their own organizations.

We invite you and your organization to join us in this vision of positively impacting a billion lives!

For questions about trainer certification, keynotes, workshops, or other training, please email us at Support@BecomingYourBest.com, call us at 888-690-8764, or visit our website at BecomingYourBest.com.

Berrett–Koehler
Publishers

Berrett-Koehler is an independent publisher dedicated to an ambitious mission: *Connecting people and ideas to create a world that works for all.*

Our publications span many formats, including print, digital, audio, and video. We also offer online resources, training, and gatherings. And we will continue expanding our products and services to advance our mission.

We believe that the solutions to the world's problems will come from all of us, working at all levels: in our society, in our organizations, and in our own lives. Our publications and resources offer pathways to creating a more just, equitable, and sustainable society. They help people make their organizations more humane, democratic, diverse, and effective (and we don't think there's any contradiction there). And they guide people in creating positive change in their own lives and aligning their personal practices with their aspirations for a better world.

And we strive to practice what we preach through what we call "The BK Way." At the core of this approach is *stewardship,* a deep sense of responsibility to administer the company for the benefit of all of our stakeholder groups, including authors, customers, employees, investors, service providers, sales partners, and the communities and environment around us. Everything we do is built around stewardship and our other core values of *quality, partnership, inclusion,* and *sustainability.*

This is why Berrett-Koehler is the first book publishing company to be both a B Corporation (a rigorous certification) and a benefit corporation (a for-profit legal status), which together require us to adhere to the highest standards for corporate, social, and environmental performance. And it is why we have instituted many pioneering practices (which you can learn about at www.bkconnection.com), including the Berrett-Koehler Constitution, the Bill of Rights and Responsibilities for BK Authors, and our unique Author Days.

We are grateful to our readers, authors, and other friends who are supporting our mission. We ask you to share with us examples of how BK publications and resources are making a difference in your lives, organizations, and communities at www.bkconnection.com/impact.

Dear reader,

Thank you for picking up this book and welcome to the worldwide BK community! You're joining a special group of people who have come together to create positive change in their lives, organizations, and communities.

What's BK all about?

Our mission is to connect people and ideas to create a world that works for all.

Why? Our communities, organizations, and lives get bogged down by old paradigms of self-interest, exclusion, hierarchy, and privilege. But we believe that can change. That's why we seek the leading experts on these challenges—and share their actionable ideas with you.

A welcome gift

To help you get started, we'd like to offer you a **free copy** of one of our bestselling ebooks:

www.bkconnection.com/welcome

When you claim your **free ebook**, you'll also be subscribed to our blog.

Our freshest insights

Access the best new tools and ideas for leaders at all levels on our blog at ideas.bkconnection.com.

Sincerely,

Your friends at Berrett-Koehler